LALIA

Lalia

POEMS

Adam Cornford

CHAX

2021

For my family,
living and dead,
to whom I owe so much

ISBN: 978-1-946104-27-4
Library of Congress Control Number: 2020943172

Chax Press
1517 N Wilmot Rd no. 264
Tucson Arizona 85712-4410

Chax Press books are supported in part by individual donors and by sales of books. Please visit *https://chax.org/membership-support/* if you would like to contribute to our mission to make an impact on the literature and culture of our time.

Contents

ALEPHS

A for Andromeda: A Poetics

for Patrick Dunagan

The poem: Gift or artifice? Message or machine? An old argument.

In the 1961 BBC TV serial *A for Andromeda*, scripted by Fred Hoyle, radio astronomers pick up a very long, repeated signal in high-speed binary code from a source in the constellation of that name. This code turns out to be instructions for assembling a computer far more powerful and sophisticated than any yet made on earth, with unknown capabilities.

Once built, the enormous computer exerts telepathic control over one of the scientists who has built it via a pair of powerful electromagnetic field generators. Compelled to grasp these terminals, she is fatally electrocuted; but not before her DNA is analyzed by the computer, which then prints out instructions for growing a humanoid clone from a genome it has designed.

This clone (played by Julie Christie in her first starring role) reaches physical maturity in weeks and is telepathically programmed by the giant computer as a brilliant mathematician and geneticist. She in turn instructs the eager, hapless bureaucrats and national-security types in how to build yet more powerful computers, which will design yet more clones, with the promise that they will provide all sorts of scientific and technological gifts.

A lone scientist realizes that this is in fact the start of an invasion of earth by alien minds encrypted into the computer code, who will occupy the cloned bodies. Superhumanly intelligent, they will first dominate our species and then replace it. Luckily, the prototype clone girl has genetic flaws that are causing her to become ill; and her body-generated human emotions make her vulnerable and cause her to betray her masters.

Together the rebellious scientist and the dying clone, whom he has named Andromeda, destroy the computer and "save humanity." The scientist, who has fallen in love with Andromeda, is left waiting to see if her life can be saved. She recovers, no longer an alien but a human woman at once naive and wise.

The radio telescope: your attention. The coded message: an associative polysemic pattern or image of truth. The giant computer: your technique. The scientist who dies: your original impulse to write. The programmed and unstable clone: the new gestalt made in the process of writing; or, if you prefer, your muse. The bureaucrats: your narcissism. The rebel scientist: your ever-unsatisfied desires. Andromeda following her cure and humanization: the poem after revision. The aliens: your true selves on the far side of language.

The poem: Organic automaton or flawed instruction set? Defeated invasion or frustrated evolution?

Initial Singularity

for Samuel Delany

Before even silence is uttered
Zeus is a point particle
Of infinite energy, infinite mass
Until his will's widthless rod
Of lightning defines direction
And Athene slides out of him,
Flat as her shield, endless as π
From her, then, ingenuity
Unfolds like a bronze rose
Whose petals razor the hand

Avowals

for Harryette Mullen

Compasses trace radius, arc, their way
away across wave crests charted, laid
to horizon, between dark spars and sails
blood constellations, arrayed rays, astral
angles navigated: archaic face to sky, his
unslave gaze takes aim at red rising day

E

Screeches to speed, to retreat, a speech of
yellow beaks wide and reaching tongues
fleeing between trees, of black wingbeats
into green, where tiered screens of leaves
shelter eggshells from shot, repeat, the pellet
echoes hissing, melting in heave of breeze

I

High iron, rising toward gray-white sky
like a machine giant's oxidized thigh-bone
perpendicular in crisscross of cables, crane—
will's wished individual liftoff as inked
upstroke, multiplied to forest, *my* and *my*
and *my*—singularity's own inlighting lie

O

Grow, slow-motion opening of hearing,
circle of known sound, of owed routine—
grow past dog-barks, past reiterate drops
on roof; round up to dome, to a cloud globe
unbounded, omnivocalic throat of Now,
to white-fount Word, o other pole of zero

U

Muse: her upraised arms, her back undulant
in dance as her tongue in outcry, then as her
uvula in murmur to whom she's urging; show
a She, smooth as tulip, unfurling unstemmed
a dew-starred universe, multiverse, closeless
truth of *you*, all ways plural, thus always Us

Angelology & Demonology

with Andrew Joron, demonologist supreme

The angel of gravity drops me down an infinite shaft at whose bottom I spread, God-oil, into an infinite circle.

Figures running in reverse—clouds, equations, sacred texts—converge upon a place foretold by the demon of abandonment.

The angel of dice fills the sky with negative constellations; there is a pattern to their pivoting no-one can determine.

La Penultième est morte: invocation of the demon of analogy.

The angel of triangles rotates me through the cardinal points: loser, keeper, and lost. My face appears to shift like wax at each displacement, but only the light changes.

The sirens of Beauty and the sirens of Emergency are one and the same, according to the demon of the air.

The angel of news impregnates us with separation's gluey sperm; we give birth to an immense grey simulacrum called Necessity.

Information's body, eaten from within. Every signal relies on—folds back—the redundancy that chance chants. Devorations of the devotions of the demon without a name.

The angel of surgery wears a body made of clean red arcs.

By a neat-fingered trick, the coolest vapors may be segregated from the warmest in a sealed chamber; the dark brain may be lighted again, if left to the care of Maxwell's demon.

The angel of repetition gives a single cry that echoes along the endless vault of his throat, having died long before his utterance is heard.

Predations that pre-date the predicate of Time, whose residue is the rosy dew of dying suns, are committed by the demon with the head of an angel.

The angel of helium juggles her halo of needles with the absolute calm that inflates the moment of extinction.

Do not listen to messages propagated by invisible means through the aether. Voices that issue from telephones, radios, and other devices, no matter how familiar and how trusted, are the mimicry of demons.

The angel of denial whispers behind dark trees at the shores of reflection: *The sky's image has no roots.*

An angle of vision is twisted into the shape of an angel by the demon of perspective.

The angel of families is a blacksmith driving us into a hoof; only our faces, flattened into mirrors for stones, remain outside the curve of belonging.

Pinned like a butterfly to the table of taxonomy, its wings still waving feebly, is the shadow of the mind: pending further examination, it will be labeled either an "angel" or a "demon."

The angel of weeping drills tiny oceans in the snow.

Commas are inserted between everyday objects, semi-colons between moments of doubt; colons are placed before the abyss: a period marks the end of Time. These are signatures of the demon of continuum.

The angel of revenge tears bread between his teeth, bread he scatters like the future as soon as we invoke him.

A poem, unlike a proposition of logic, cannot be refuted. But there is a light that leaks slowly from its edges, and it empties. The words remain, perhaps, but they grow still. The thoughts of a demon are no different.

The angel of presence batters down the door but leaves it intact, marked with the Aleph, the throat's hesitation before speech .

Lects

Where Late

for Philip Lamantia

Their former numerousness I begin to imagine
especially when rain welds to small dark berries
and the sky is flush-layered and scattered early
with the old swollen sun's effort in descending:
How their converse would have surrounded me

walking across short native grasses now exiled
or through conspiring reeds or under live-oaks'
digression—their queries, their volute repeated
assertions of *am*, announcements of going and
return, flared warnings and chants of longing—

All this a mosque of chaotic filigree around me
drawn together by their quick lines of motion:
So many gathered in redwood minarets looking
down as from dusty windows of light, so many
settling in the meadows' clefts and shadow-tents,

so many whose vision-brain joins two worlds as
their bodies join two wings about heart's power,
so many who know the air's layers and savors
as a swimmer water's moods under sun-mask,
so many afloat above inlets, diving among pines—

I imagine before our walls and ways, hearing
their phrases unstrippable still to mere signals
I would have walked as a beast among beasts, a
mind among minds in thicket-sounding twilight,
that starred utterance talking the night down

Jargon

for Ronald Johnson

"translucent, colorless, or smoky"

                           like *jacinth*, a kind of zircon

"the inarticulate utterance of"

                                 the birdes that jargonned on the ryver

                                       that *made her to sleepe*

(from the *Metamorphosis*)

"to utter by warbling, warble"   a child's water-whistle bird-call

        to sing because one cannot speak

              what one knows

                     birdwoman, birdman, dark-feathered as the oaks

        singing wings to each other

                                      under hook'd moon

"a jingle or assonance of rhymes"

                   warble, chatter, jabber, twitter

"to talk unintelligibly"

"nonsense, gibberish" as the *idiot* with private tongue

        babble-canting of the manic, rhyme-blur slangs of the dangerous

jargon, jangle, jugementis falce

              we know it when we hear it   because we don't know it

"a cipher, or other system of characters

having an arbitrary meaning"

             encrypted, hidden in Alterity's wet branch-vaults

(metamorphosis)   most hateful those family words looking away

          from us, long-kidnapped children who

                     raised by savages, will not now look us in the eye

"barbarous, rude, or debased"

       barbari, those who make animal sounds, meaning

                         a speech over the Empire's talk-horizon

      heard from around song-fires deep   in the roadless forest

            songs ancestors of those to be sung

               in trashed marble villas   a few centuries later

"hybrid speech arising from a mixture of languages"

English, for instance, that trader's pidgin   rutted mud-track
                    of Old Norse, Anglo-Saxon, Latin fragments
          rain-dotted diphthongs slanting down
(metamorphosis)   from the moss-moors dissolving the gutturals, pulping
                    inflection's leaves to skeleton traces underwheel
          syntax of hoofprints moving away

                                                  down the forest road
                    centuries later
"applied contemptuously"
                              as these quotes like prim black forceps
"to a 'lingo'"
"to any mode of speech abounding in unfamiliar terms:"
"of scholars or philosophers" the *aporia*, the *chiasmus*:

                                                  crossings through void

"of science or art" the *penumbra*, the *chiaroscuro*:

shadows alight
"of a class, trade, or profession" the *wildcat*, the *holiday*, the *synapse*:

                                         openings where the New

     arcs

                through crystalline space

                              "smoky, colorless,

translucent"
        meaning
                  as the blackbird's quick wave-packet   *my nested oak*
                      the owl's cool lift-off   *my hunting air*
                          the lark's arabesque at zenith   *my solar heart*

       but to those out of the know, the talk-circle
"a medley or babel of sounds"
                   shim, kluge, metsat, leadfoot, bronk, knockdown, cob

that savage jargon of yells, brays, or screams
familiarly yet feebly termed 'the cries of —'

       all which by meaning nothing to You, means Us
the birdes that jargonned on the ryver
       (glints on the move, eddies and whorls print-patterned at the margin)
       singing, water-calling
(metamorphosis)   in this city of trees, of towers
                                   that have never

ceased to fall

Bonus Killville

for Lindsay Hill

Some woofwoof with a torso is you, clambers the risk tubes and ruby ledges.

Hopscotching under thunderstones, he drop-kicks bomb-boxes, a high number.

Dodgy round the dayglow snarlbot, then punch it topside into new point-stars.

Burlyboy boings after you on updown drums, you jump to risers only, lose him.

An easy skate across trembly white stairs of splash in this cashflow colorstream.

Then it's rollover sliders into Hammer Gardens for a grab-the-apple zigzag.

Too tooth-pink in this busy toondome for a bang-diver, so you hit Bounce!

Toddle down the bit-mist crayon moonpath plucking plus-lilies, pigtail dollyoid.

Many a polka mushroom to ding on and roll the Add register before you drop.

Keep up zap-attack when you swim him buddyless through the Lobster Lobby.

Gotta bust a zillion fangy grinners this level, hotfoot, if you don't want to X-eye.

Your squidgy earn-dragon learns to sidewind razor-rings with no helper tiki.

Fifty-plus more fireblows on the bad 'roos, so you're ported to Bonus Killville.

Whatever avatar, all slaughter-score runs mimic a grownup money-gain solo.

D.O.A.

for David Lehman

Poisoned with "luminous toxin." Slow-acting, so I wouldn't know, not at first. Now it's too late. The toxin's all through my nerves and arteries already, lighting me up inside like a neon medusa. I've got days and nights left to live. To find the answers. Who fed me the dose? And why? Who will have killed me?

Was it "A," the accountant, the numbers guy—the secret gambler whose balanced figures held my world together? He keeps crystals on his desk, he knew all the angles before they were born, he has the odds figured down to the last photon. Has he just blacked out my column in the books?

Or was it "B," the bad-good mama with the blue dress on—the babe with the cloudy eyes and the hot-iron heart? She could be smooth as air, quick as eyes in the forest, or soft as new grass. With her, though, no-one's forever. The big clock in her hips ticks like sex but strikes like a dead-bell. Did she slip me the firefly venom in a kiss?

Maybe it was "C," the cold-eyed chemist who makes a science of stopping hearts. His mind only travels one way, like Time. Is he the one who's been trailing me just out of sight, never in a hurry, watching me sweat, waiting for me to fall apart? Did he mix up the lethal light that's eating my bones?

Of course it could have been "D," Big Daddy—Mister Know-It-All, always looking down on the mortal streets from the Sky-High Suite and calling the shots. He can let you ride his elevator right to the top or send you on a one-way trip to the basement furnace. Did he order his phosphorus angel to walk in my footsteps?

Or after all was it "O," the Operator, the one behind the scenes who's seen by no-one? They call her Lady Omega, but she's as much the beginning of this story as the end. Her big shades hide the original secrets, her black phone holds all the stars. Was she the one who set me up, who lighted my road to nowhere?

Luminous toxin. It's been in me all this time. It's making me weaker, turning my hair grey, rusting my heart, even while it lights up everything I see. It's in my words too, making them glow. See, I'm smarter now that I know I'm on my way out. I've got to work fast. And you—whoever did this to me, they're coming for you next.

How I Make It: Daedalos Outside

I maker make it back to Solitude with legs bruised and paper feathers charred
my eyeballs eclipsed by an imperial sun I find myself
in the unbuilt labyrinth beyond the labyrinth I built I make it one more time
between eyeless walls following the thread stretched ahead by my desire
behind me the false palace ruined its blue halls cracked its images thrown down
I make it to Clarity ridge only to see a higher range ahead
before me a steep scramble into the everydayscape and its fog of event
I make it down

in time time slow turning overhead a Ferris-wheel of iron lights I make it
in time time a clepsydra of sweat a mill grinding the hours
into black glittering flour for the vampire lord as in the folktale
the vampire lord who today has no body but a planetary wind of ons and offs
sucking time out of our wavelet lives as a hurricane distils its cloud
I make time into the bread of sleep I spread it with the honey of caresses
I make it up the hillside like a lead feather floating backwards
like a demon moving his library out of hell one heavy burning box at a time
I make it out

from the night clouds into the dawn clouds
from Broken Valley with its webs of small-caliber hatred
its cars whirling steel zeros its park of scorched oaks and insulted grass
by way of a long ellipse above the cloudy Bay through shame's heaven and back
through phones thrown at walls doors hammered yellow shrieks and vomit
to Holdout Hill with its maps of friendly footsteps
its dog beacons its flaky grandeurs propped above the green-grown creek
its cottages sprouting new asymmetric stories or skylights for the moon
I make it over

to the warm house on legs halted above a slope of apple trees and eucalypts
the study cockpit windowed with arcades of rain in long curved leaves
with catenaries and acute angles of hummingbirds and arcs of hawks
the cockpit steering motionless into the west wind

facing the red and black shadows of ships facing
the office towers glassy stromatolites raised by Capital's primitive cells
on the San Francisco side the pale houses that feather the far shore
facing the mountain that narrows into a steel tree the Goddess of Transmission
and the blood-orange gates opening to the ocean's white fractals
and beyond them over the world-curve sinuous littoral perspectives of Asia
I make it together

with the one I love in the warm roots of the hillside
the home that was above me all this time waiting for me to kneel
at the feet of the one I love in the basement attic
full of morning or awash in moon I make it
with the one I love under the buttocks of cloud the wet eye of paradise I make it
my back a drum with many tongues I make the surrender *clave*
my skin a score blending into red unison I make the hips' counterpoint
I make it new

with the one I love walking the integrated circuits of dusk hand in hand
under the streetlamp that flicks out as we approach
with the one I love curled like an open quotation or like rain
sliding down sleep's horizontal window I make it night after night I make it
with the one I love loving the back's alluvial valley the inner thigh's
pillowy pavilions the hair's ripple the back of her neck a white door
and the four-dimensional curve of her lips entering a kiss
I make it even

with broken lightning in my knees and pebbled slopes in my footsoles I make it
even with my dandelioning hair and solar forehead I make it
even with my cracked aqueduct lips and leafless hands I make it
it helpless and bald as a baby mouse under thunderous floorboards I make
it sudden and vicious as an eel in a crevice of rotting Melanesian corals I make
it agile and tremulous as a spider-monkey fleeing bulldozers I make
it sociable and amused as a dolphin threading his maze of echoes I make
it impartial and immense as a seraph its quantum wingspread covering invisibly
every version of my city that can possibly exist and therefore does
every version of myself a humanifold radiant from the instant of my conception

I make from two half strands of DNA and all the worlds
I make it up

in my brain's caravel in the foaming bow-wave of my neocortex
in the stump of my brain's severed sternsail my speech center
I make it up in my mouth like spit and kisses
I make it in my lungs twin Babel towers of air buried among heart's blue roots
I make it in my throat a magnetic gun aimed at the full moon
I make it in my hand a neighborhood of twisted and interrupted streets
I make it on the screen letter by letter each an eightfold prayer
conveyed by kabbalah's many-winged commands into the compiler uttered
in black-white speech of assembly placed in the mosaic floor of this paradise
and returned to my gaze as in the alchemist's mirror black yet spirit-lit
I make it in your optic nerves and in the vast cumulonimbus brain of language
that overshadows your own brain linked to it in both directions
by connotation's blown drifting downpour and the blinding return stroke
I make it here

the cool wet air of April you begin to imagine as I breathe I make it
a scholar demon climbing weighed down and lifted by his smoldering wings
I make it with all the maps I make it all with her with him with you as you read
I make it here now I make it all heres all nows in which I am I maker make

Topoi

Connected

Last of all by air ceaseless tide
running the channel of my windpipe in

and out of the lungs' weedy pools
by microbial traffic filling every pore

billions living between my own
big nucleated cells those

self-replicating precision machines
like mice in a factory

vast migrations through my gut
two-way infiltrations of my skin

not just by the bacteria
whose genius is multitude and mistake

coating me inside and out
but viruses bees of RNA pollen

bring news from everywhere from
back down my short species twig

of the bushy tree of life then
past apes lemurs tree-shrews

amphibians fish trilobites
segmented worms

to the archaea building towers
around volcanic vents

in the deep hot crush of oceans
three billion years ago

Enabling me to know this
the intricate lichen-folds of my neocortex

connect with a great invisible forest
language the semiotic multiverse

through ears eyes and fingertouch
on this machine to planetary networks

and before all else the quantum
fields that are every atom

boson lepton I consist of
trading light and spreading

out to the ever-vanishing horizon
of the universe with diminishing odds

of me being anywhere but here
alone in a house in the desert

Corridors

The corridors of time branch endlessly, each consequence calyx opening into countless others,
   like bouquets of subway tunnels under the city of the Possible.

The shock corridor, though enameled and tiled white, smells of old shit and lightning. It is
   littered with the torn-off pinions of Oblivion's angels.

In the corridors inside the Great Pyramid, Pythagoras, reborn as a worm with a luminous head,
   crawls through a tetrahedral peach of eroded stone.

Over the war maps hover corridors of air. The missile drones slide along them, silver
   raindrops across the window of the commander's limousine.

Van Gogh's Arles asylum corridor sways like a rope bridge over his grief ravine, under the
   white receding arches of days that block out the stars.

The kiss is a corridor worn smooth by water: at its bottom, the unseen well-pool where my
   tongue, a fleshy reflection, dances with its origin.

In the corridor of peripheral vision, doors open silently on either side. There on the left,
   was that the stained-glass hand of summer twilight beckoning?

Laughter runs crowding up the throat corridor, children getting out from dissecting
   incongruities in class who now scatter in the playground's milky air.

The gray tile corridors of George Tooker cross at angles like prisms of isolation, splitting
   paired stares from each other, doubling the sadness of overcoats and shoes.

Along my blood's corridors I move unrecognized among crimson wheels and wolves
   of glass. Viruses flash me signals, teaching me how to be a different animal.

Down Francis Bacon's corridor every fisheyed room shows glandular stimulus and wet response:
   the skinbags twist naked, smearing their routine screams.

At the far end of the corridors of Renaissance perspective with their checkered tiles and frozen gestures, a singularity in which perfection vanishes.

The stepped corridors of my brain wind around each other. Each ends in a chamber of Babel's library, its lights flickering, doors wide in all directions.

Along corridors with mirrored walls races a single photon like a white-haired girl. Past the double doors, her countless versions collapse breathless into one.

Forbidden Planet

for Alexandria Volk

A call for help is addressed to the future, but which future will answer?

Blind but crowded with eyes, the gigantic lens outpaces light.

Even now, manhood is grey, good-humored, and efficient.

To re-enter time, we must stand silent inside columns of glass.

Beneath us, an absence of cities and the idea of cities.

Far from its origin, a branch breaks off the tree of instructions.

Radio: to refuse help, to warn (to threaten), to guide (to threaten).

Descent into a landscape defined by jagged renderings of the sublime.

The alchemist automaton, quick with forces, slow in gait and speech.

Total suburb: house built on limitless energy, property circled by limitless absence.

A philosophy can shut its eyes when its garden becomes menacing.

The survivor hides his innocence from strangers and his guilt from himself.

Doorways, like coffins, reveal the proportions of the always inhuman dead.

To speak: to perform magic using vast apparatus one has neither designed nor understood.

The receding vistas of technology, where power flows from the vanishing point.

Three impulses in young women: befriending wild animals; flirting; fashion.

All objects contain great generators, mysterious motions, deep shafts into fire.

A mirror that needs a mirror in which to see itself without seeing death.

To lift weights without using one's muscles, to assemble a child from sparks.

The tiger of wrath disintegrated by the horseman of instruction.

Murder is a product of evolution, its body a product of invention.

Reason asleep produces monsters, but only when its logic is left on.

Becoming visible in the force-fields of male fear, female desire.

Understanding washed away by its own carrier-wave of light.

Your will presses its burning name through every door you close against it.

Death: all the dials gone red, infinite energy meeting itself head on.

The bride with her bachelors leaves her father bare as a star.

Little Nemo: Know No One Wonderland

for David Meltzer

Your bed rises on wooden tentacles and stalks off into window-severed night

The night reaches down cloudhooks to grapple papa's prosperous brownstone

Your brownstone slowly explodes in a shower of carved mahogany and velvet

The mahogany and velvet reverse-film themselves into a serpentine Pullman car

The Pullman car starlit plunges with you across shadowy meadows of rooftops

Meadows of rooftops weedy with laundry seed countless grinning balloons

These grinning balloons cluster up into brain-berries bigger than church bells

The brain-berries chime in ragtime behind silenced mulatto eggs dancing in line

The silenced eggs whip on their minstrel masks and burst their lip-stitches

Their lip-stitches unfurl past your stare braiding cables of the Brooklyn Bridge

The Brooklyn Bridge rears in showers of suicides to become a flickery colonnade

This colonnade mirrors itself into a four-dimensional railroad-trust palazzo

The palazzo turns inside out to surround you with a forest of lantern cages

The lantern cages release silk caterpillars to be needled by Hassidic wasps

Some Hassidic wasps hear tiger-lily trombones and go onstage as butterflies

These butterflies your mama's petticoats are sewn into a silken white airship

The white airship gets lost among apes in Brooklyn's polygonal perspectives

Brooklyn's perspectives break up into ice-floes of tangled sheets and pillows

The ice-floes arch a labyrinth where your gasp shatters the translucent princess

The princess spins into a rose-window that showers you with handbill petals

The petals grow lacy edges and flutter down as Valentines with red eyes

These red-eyed Valentines offer circuses and stock quotes to shrewd seagulls

The seagulls discover over rainy piers the hypnotic staircase of their wings

The gull-wing staircase spirals you calling out dream-secrets down to your bed

Stelae

for the exploited dead of New York and the world, September 2001

giant stelae side by side
grave markers to dead work
vertical crystals grown
from solution of millions
of used hours ocean of
hands eyes repeating same
motions facing machine
motions as life streams out
traded for never enough
rice masa water space
for never enough world
and inside in layered air
more hands eyes voices
repeat inside the cubes
pass the lost hours on add
their own flowed in wires
logic gates behind screens
floor on floor of numbers
down to nucleic strings
of Is and Os of eyes and
mouths open flowed flown
on the way to build power
of enormous wings of fire
bombs brain bombs of towers
taller over the work city
more as each life lessens

giant towers side by side
glass columns of live breath
fifty-two thousand hearts
counting in layered air
flaring of all those brains
alight with numbers jokes
repeated between cubes
eye motions face machine
logic as life streams out
hands eyes open wider
enormous wings break in
then fire bursts like veins
through walls paper skin
some living descend hand
in hand blind in the beams
some seen flown in last air
smoke tower grave marker
built before its dead can die
their burnt hands eyes work
make its grey swirl stone
stele that swallows itself
as the death city inhales
the dead work towers built
in reverse time grey lapse
millions of hours now
ash fall never to be lived

Blue Drift

sky after storm, September 14, 2001

Pale head-scumble and mushroom cluster along slip scuppers

Smudge assemblies tower below into a slowing tornado claw

Horse-island processional between fossil roof and tumbletown

A palm-octopus dilates its dark points under long heave-hulls

Sway of shade ribs like subway lines in a vague skin skein

A skeleton puffsnake underbites the river's slate-shade belly

Long slide-glide trails veils across the warped angel wreckage

One sputter-train eases by through a streamy repeater tunnel

Volt cross-rods stammer as the flecked skins blue into merge

Fainting bronze-gray drapes trail down after fadeout sunfall

Fool's Paradise

Same cumulus   cordilleras   violet shadows   in the distance

as you glide

     pivot   through your   new freedom

same

     archipelagoes   of rust-gold cirrus

     tufted
     with   same

smoke-palms   evanescent foliage

     where you pass

leaning   your head back   singing
     your laughter

     joins the wind's   eleisons

and just beyond

     the horizon   of your vision

cool

     joyous murmur in   your ears

the Saved   drifting inside   vertical gardens
     solar aureoles

     are really there

different   from you

     only in this

     that gravity   has not

     forgotten   you

as you   make your   way
wingless

     leisurely   accelerating

     toward the center
     of the earth

Spatial Jazz

"All human locomotion is controlled falling" —T. Dickinson

Inwheeling to a jump-flower of all hands
We swing mechanicals in clock windows
A sly deference under slow slide and lift
Shale twists, a waking geology breath,
A happy slumber slump we twist to hitch
Where's base of this hook retract and away?
Pivot the little between hip-bounce links
Fold this bib-ship into a long wing clicking
Heart machine flips in and out, the gnarl-tree
Ape-leaps and heave wave into happy racket
Planet-runners haste round the Ha!-snarler
Black parasol saucers through a fall of stars
Crows down, their ark-arc raffle and smack—
Eclipse dome, scurry of wiggle flares to stop

for Theresa Dickinson and the ZaZa dancers

Montezuma Castle

ruins near Sedona, Arizona

This close canyon worn in pre-Cambrian ocean floor
layer under layer of pale diatom shells fallen slowly
through then pressed by wet cold tons far below light
into chalky rock thrust up to plateau four thousand feet
spread bare to raindrift and to slide and sleight of wind
canyon slow cut by snow spate river knuckled below
white sycamores that widen fine boughs into antennae

Between lime strata serpents undulant in the cliff face
ridged with block teeth rows like Mayan skull glyphs
rise tiers of smooth square-windowed rose mud walls
Here the departed No-Water people hung warm homes
like the swallows whose nest holes pock around where
grain store crawlspace caves gap the soft off-white stone

Within they wove baskets of X arrays and radial zigzags
cut yucca with black glass ground corn on granite wheels
Up and down long stick socketed ladders bound with gut
they could raise quick against bear cougar or flash flood
to where their fires tinted inside walls to clay-red flicker
And always traveling sky past the cliff's crumbled lip
slow wind waves washing rain clouds or snow clouds
ghosts of the fallen sea over river chant and raven call

Town six hundred years empty now the why unknown
unheard their names for themselves and their flute songs

High Desert Rest Prayer

(Arizona, February 2009)

Calm to the heart's double drum in the ribcage kiva

Calm to the swishing willows of the lungs

Calm to the tongue poised and tense as a lizard in its crevice

Calm to the eyes that will hatch the birds of dream

Calm to the bones like arrows in the skin's quiver

Calm to the brain that cliff-dwelling of ten thousand rooms

Calm to the restless half-curled spiders of the hands

Calm to the ears the secret burial chambers of music

Calm to the feet those doors hinging between earth and air

Calm to the gut that rippling underground river

Calm to the body under the snowy witnessing moon

Calm to the body under the beaded winter stars

Calm to the body resting on its journey to calm

Calm to the body

Calm to the body

Calm carry the body to the reedy pool of sleep

Spaces Inside Sleep

for Robert Desnos

Never a new building now I'm inside, none of the sudden modern houses
with invisible walls and white inner balconies, only grimed stone or pale timbers—

—grey plank walls and beams under peeling paint in a vast warehouse built
around a lake steaming with phantoms, we have to traverse it on catwalks
to reach tall doors dilating onto the grassy downs where fire-balloons rise—

—boards of a splintering floor in a shadow-store abandoned, its basement
stacked with moldering foam pillows a space where I find myself partway
out of myself a mirror-space that shows me another me, younger, light-haired
in loose linen shirt and flowered vest floating up iron stairs to be admired—

—a vague toyshop displaying grainy carved puppets in carnival dress
at the back a plywood-lined staircase reveals itself leading to the attic of my childhood
that house hanging behind the dream like a shadowbox in which are suspended
brass microscopes, postcards, conjuror's boxes, tiles painted with birds, lithographs
of perspective and of course my own lantern faces multiplying at the windows—

—the square worn-cobbled courtyard of a castle where I sit on steps
among the others rejoicing as my "unreal" son discovers with a few strokes
of his five-year-old fingers on the lute I've given him the whole chord of his future
and where a seeming young woman whose smile stretches inhumanly pursues me
along colonnades over tiled or leaded rooftops as she pokes and claws me
in glee with many-jointed extensible carved arms knowing I cannot escape her—

—a crumbling art-deco hotel overlooking the harbor, its once Aegean blue
or jade-green paintwork chipped winks with pale plaster, its wide front windows
embrace advancing navies of cumulo-nimbus, the typhoon sweeps blurred strollers
off the esplanade the guests are screaming, tumbling behind frayed grey divans
as blown pinwheels of ice intricate as mandalas burst the plate glass inward
and I seize the hand of my "real" son, running him along blind hallways, down
stairwells awash with storm-light into a bare stone cellar where I hold him safe—

These untrustworthy leaves of wood and mineral spread above the years
I will spend lying on my side in the dark arranging meetings with the once-desired
the feared or the dead—forest canopy over ever more life-branches unfollowed,
a knotted and hinged or mortared foliage of uncertainty trembling in the wind
of my sleeping breath as I roll and drift along the pale road toward waking
and toward the instant when these unreeling variations, frame by frame interior
opening into still shakier half-repaired and wish-littered interior, are abruptly
stopped, and the eroded wreckage tumbles up into new cities of stars

Red Venice

for Y.F.

Dans Venise le rouge/ Ni un cheval bouge (In red Venice/ Not a horse is moving)
—Alfred de Musset, written before he had seen Venice

In solitary London
all the stone steps are connected

In brave Accra
dolls float in the lagoons

In silent Munich
night has a long tongue

In drifting Chicago
iron hammers fall slowly

In ascendant Minneapolis
the tall mirrors have wheels

In frozen Paris
children can breathe tulle

In fragrant Ulan Baatar
knife-grinders hymn the moon

In crenellated Mumbai
craneflies invite thunder

In shiny Dallas
a rooster screams among certainties

In bored Asuncion
the bishop dissects a virgin

In vacant Shanghai
acrobats own the streets

In luminous Harare
only obsidian has wings

In blue Santiago de Cuba
no moths are arrested

In crystalline Akron
willows bend to the crows

In ghostly Novgorod
great mantids tiptoe

In muscular Rome
apartments open like books

In smooth Cuernavaca
a wind-spirit caresses herself

The Green Star

after Lin Carter

As the green star rises
      we runaways from Steel Planet wake

                         in branching shadow
                under
          the green star we
descend   below lawn-wide leaves into   expanded origin

Green star, engine of transmutation glowing in every cell, let us take passage on your Green Star Line

     As the green star
rises
     lemur tongues inscribe
           death-script around   porticos of bark
a snail-car trailing silk
           steam traverses
               midforest aisles

Green star, attractor of the currents of leaves, the fractals of insects, draw us into your viridian spiral

     As the green
          star rises
photosynthesis enters
         the syntax of
               our chameleon skin
          under the green
                  star
thorn-spear warriors   poise like the mantis in   jetée

Green star, Word for the forest-world, green thought above green night, let our love grow vaster than empires

As the green star
                rises
day   filters down through
            layers   of shade   but never
to the wet root arcades
                    whose amphibian herds   and hundred-legged
                                                        tigers perceive it only
                            as heat

Green star, end of the world-woods, whose woods are between worlds, whose glades are doors and diagrams, amaze us

        As the green
                            star rises
moss-furred
                angels ascend in   a cloud from
                                        endless crowns just
above where   jade
                        gourds are homes   to waking
            dragonfly-riders

Green star, demiurge of heliotropics, of sunwalking banyans and sequoias, vine us with lightning's logic

        As the green
                            star rises
in hanging   cities
        gardens of
                    masks ripen to   reptilian twilight
            under the green
                    star
script of
        serpents, grammar   of boughs,
                                bird-metaphors

Green star, the trees climb their own bodies toward you, hands outstretched, leaves gazing upward, let them arrive as we have

      As

            the green star rises

the world radiates

                 trees, the star forests

                                   itself with light

in aloe-smooth

            faces, our eyes

               flower

                    with the inhuman

Green star, eye of the Green Man, the hunter crowned with branch–antlers, each of them reaching into another life, gaze on your prey

Gravity's Angels

after Feynman, "Universal Gravitation: An Example of Physical Law"

To make us travel along closed curves, ellipses
as Kepler understood, angels were needed.

The tireless beat of their wings on space, of their angular feathers
pushes all worlds together.
So many angels, we mistake them for clouds
furring the planet's curvature,
its cone of shadow their wake as they press inward against sunlight.

Nothing desires to fall, to converge. It wants to keep going.
Angels lean us into our seats and shoes, tug our skins downward,
lead us toward the center of the earth, after so many years of falling
into scalding nickel-iron cores of each other—

God made the angels. The angels
assembled galaxies, then stars, then planets. All the while,
though, hidden inside the atom-hells, unpredictable demons worked
hunched over. Inside the twisted and splintered space
God left behind for them after the very start of things
they bind sullen-browed nuclei, frantic electrons
leaping away like souls toward connection.

Crushed wasplike in the cores of suns, tumbled through nebulae
demons are water's architects, and snow's; they sculpt the proteins; they
the nerve-gardeners, foresters in bone. And all the while
stars go through their graceful motions, the moon
falls faultlessly past the horizon every time. Angels
get all the credit.

God (with regret) made the demons. The demons make worlds
out of infinitesimal crisscross of force, flame-blur of probability.
He made the angels. The angels

push worlds together, making them drop
away from the straight lines they were traveling in,
into God's finely, dully differential loops.

Where they were trying to go and why, till the angels took over
not even God, the single true Circle, understands.
That unknowing is his only circumference. Sometimes
along that sensitive edge, He feels a straight line, widthless and burning
coldly, to Him: like O of absolute zero uncurled into infinity's
I, tangent at every point to His arc, it's a highway
where a Traveler is always already passing, on the move
from before the beginning, to after the end—

To See the Black Angel

at the time of the assault on Gaza, 2008–9

To see the Black Angel
not descending from heaven
but risen still incandescent
out of the earth's core
and the opening of Hell
swan-diving upward
a neural fire-arrow
through the sullen mantle
and ancient sea-bed
then the villages and stones
of Palestine Israel
leaving a hollow stem of glass
like lightning's return stroke
a gush of terrene blood
in the shape of a woman

To see the Black Angel
cooling as she ascends
over scrub trees and low hills
scatters of wreckage
burnt-out trucks
eviscerated homes
fragments of char and bone
brass and depleted uranium
broken asphalt
then layers of night air
thermals upthrusting
into the Father's cool vault
slow-motion drift of planets
freeze-frame of galaxies

To see the Black Angel
as her wings widen
feathered with overlaid night
glinting like Aztec blades
She soars over the cities of men
cooling to perfect black
black smooth as obsidian
agile as latex remorseless as iron
streamlined as orca
her hair long streamers of ink
her eyes fumaroles
her breasts like the spaces
around a star's core
her sex a singularity
parting like a seed
into new physical laws
her lips in a terrible smile

To see the Black Angel
swinging a flail of sparks
as she swoops low over rooftops
Her flail reaches down
fine bright as medusa tendrils
through sleeping ceilings
of tenements and shelters
into beds into bodies
Women stir beside men
as the fire-knots brush them
From the midpoint of their spines
behind the solar plexus
news travels in all directions
up to the brain and its eyes
down to the womb
out to the callused feet
the meticulous fingers

To see the Black Angel
watching the women's skulls
room by room street by street
hut by shack by torn tent
strung lanterns fluxing with glow
as cortical zones become active
designs for infernal machines
sketched in neon 3-D
as their vulvas flicker
into fuchsias of wet flame
their hips remember to be palaces
their hearts flex and stretch
immense paradoxical demons
winged with violet vessels
To see the Black Angel
passing over all sparing none
so the women dream
of smiles like dark birds
on their lips girl-full
mother-pursed or crone-fissured
They dream of men kneeling
begging forgiveness
of tears in men's eyes like a tide
as the Angel passes over
of knives fallen like leaves
machine-pistols and RPGs
abandoned among the stones
by the Father's armies

To see the Black Angel
with the terrible smile
her flail knotted with light
making the women dream
of filling the streets
immense flocks of birds
crowding over the rubble

over stain-maps of blood
past cars twisted scorched
the skulls of dogma
they dream of governments
and parties imploding
like bomb-struck buildings
blast waves in reverse
time's arrow like the Angel
flung back from the Omega

To see the Black Angel
passing over moving on
as the women dream of power
and of waking to make it
they dream of all the lords
lords of oil and mirrors
of smoke and water
lords of light and money
of love and shadow

in Tel Aviv Washington
London Beijing Riyadh
of all these lords descended
by sighing elevators
from their armored heavens
shrunk into men trembling
in expensive rags
as all those they used for so long
dance with mouths open
drinking solar wine

To see the Black Angel
when Hell reclaims the world
as a forest of branching flame
a garden of unbound spirits
every leaf every root holy
under the oxygen eyes

of Gaia into whose body
the Angel has returned
black as abandoned veils
as the inside of touch
a drop of black ink
abruptly silvered
by a four-dimensional mirror
in the shape of a woman
a woman striding
taller than thought itself
whose face reflects the unbounded
in the faces of all
the living on earth

Oración

por René Yáñez

Nuestra Senõra del Tiempo arreglado y poderoso
Virgen transparente con lágrimas de vidrio preciso
Hija de los ritmos de brazos inumerables y anónimos
y de los ascensores en los centros financieros
delante de nosotros te avanzas siempre más allá
en tu vientre inmanchable no llevas un salvador
sino un reloj lunar con manos de avispas negras
que nos pican minuto por minuto inyectándonos
con sus larvas hambrientos de experiencias
      Entumécenos

Nuestra Señora del Tiempo aritmético y final
Virgen coronada por nanosegundos radiantes
Hija de la explosión de poblacion de ángeles
sobre la punta blanca de calor del alfiler de Diós
delante de nosotros te retiras siempre más allá
mirándonos con tus ojos cámaras oscuras digitales
qué triste tu sonrisa como la tarde ahumada
sobre miles de coches retrasadas en filas
sus conductores tan separadas como galaxias
      Jubílanos

Nuestra Señora del Tiempo termodinámico
Virgen con tu sexo una predicción arrugada
Hija de la velocidad de luz y del carbón silencioso
Madre del artrítis y de agujeros en el cerebro
del trabajo como ellos en un pan estrellada de ojos
inmóvil tu te mueves delante de nosotros siempre
más allá como el horizonte de la supervivencia
mientras nos encierras en el cielo destellante
del desperdicio medido es decir del dinero
      Olvídanos

Prayer

(English version by the author)

Our Lady of Time ordered and powerful time
Transparent Virgin with accurate glass tears
Daughter of the rhythms of countless anonymous arms
and of rhythms of elevators in financial centers
before us you advance ever further away
in your stainless belly you carry no savior
but a moon-clock with hands of black wasps
that pierce us minute by minute injecting us
with their hungry larvae of experience
        Numb us

Our Lady of Time arithmetical final time
Virgin crowned with radiant nanoseconds
Daughter of the population explosion of angels
on the white-hot point of God's needle
before us you retreat ever further away
watching us with digital camera obscura eyes
how sad your smile is like the smoky dusk
over thousands of cars held up in lines
their drivers as separate as galaxies
        Retire us

Our Lady of Time thermodynamic time
Virgin with your sex a crumpled forecast
Daughter of the speed of light and silent carbon
Mother of arthritis and of gaps in the brain
of work like the ones in bread starred with eyeholes
unmoving you move ahead of us always
further away like survival's horizon
while you enclose us in the glittering heaven
of measured waste in other words money
        Forget us

The Time Famine

for Dennis Hayes

Like the bellies of famine children, who
sitting dully on fissured earth have
nothing but time and almost no time at all,
our days have distended,

and like those children
we hunger surrounded by overflowing
prices as swiftly digital as rice,
as memoryless and purposeful as water—

but not like, because we've forgotten
we're waiting for the glinting grain of life
or the dark meal of sleep, that we
agreed to wait, not like them because

our waiting is busy as the flies round their eyes,
crowded with quick articulate workings,
with appetite's mouth-parts
ticking, with a muffled buzz like instinct;

so that hunger in us is not
implosive emptiness but implanted
growth, a larva lengthening segments
under the swollen curve of our lives:

coiled like a mainspring, eyeless
but gleaming with intent, it eats
precisely, muscle-mass, nerve, then on
to the vitals one at a time; it cleans us

to slumped sacs awash in
screenlight, hung in feeder tubes; and having
reserved the will's red fist for last, slips out
of our open mouths and moves on.

Ode to Water

for the Water Protectors

Origin,
immanent
aleph of life,
colorless
thief of the spectrum,
translucent as spirit,
we are inside you
as you are inside us,
deep and deeper
sidereal blue,
ocean's green malachite,
repeated
in the lungs and intestines.
Primeval and mineral
you fill the womb
where the embryo grows
like the first archaea
under a sky of blood.
You fill our hearts,
red moons
that drive the double tide
through our arteries
through dense mangroves of muscle
to the shores of the skin.
You replenish
the green distilleries
of rose and redwood,
you ascend inside cornstalks
like filaments of light
and thread the oak's
lichened labyrinth,
you bathe the delicate feet of rice
and the heron's claws

as you travel always
where the planet sends you.

Water,
you fall in trillions
of vertical mirrors
from cloud cordilleras,
you spin down, tiny cogwheels
toothed with ice
in winter's machine,
then you ascend again
from morning leaves,
from the map's mirrored veins,
from the sea's laboring shoulders,
from our breath.
How could we ever
exhaust you?
How could we, your children,
torture and scar
your immense
four-dimensional
seraphic body?

But that's what we're doing,
water, all of us
trapped like you
in capital's everyday circuits,
passing you
through the pipes
of stupidity factories,
shitting and sweating
into your clarity
the black ash of power,
tarry greed-sludge,
trapping you
in overheated sky
as violent clouds,

garotting you
with razor-wire molecules,
souring your currents
with carbon-charred air
so that your undulant
miles-wide
oxygen gardens choke
and the great reef cities
become their own ghosts—

No more.

Now water stands up
in us, ocean ascendant
on bone masts and spars,
in arterial rigging,
we water defy
the iron-sheathed black snakes
pumping their corpse-tar
into the mouths of deep springs,
blinding the rivers,
we water millions
flow chanting through cities,
we water drain out of offices,
warehouses, terminals,
flood bare marble capitols,
break in unceasing waves
against the armored
machines of the Poisoners,
the Makers of Desert,
we water rise,
we water rush over
and around, we water
break through
and wash away.

and with thanks to Pablo Neruda

The Air Waves

I recall as I wait for her call the RKO Pictures tower
thousands of miles tall a colossus of black girders
astride the North Pole of the radio-shrunken globe
sending out concentric ripples of Morse code R-K-O
How radio masts in Betty Boop and Popeye cartoons
shot big zigzag waves of signal down into the sets
each console flailing and bouncing with the music
amid the rubbery furniture of cartoon living rooms
stretching their speaker grilles into toothy mouths to yell
the announcer's excitement or the demagogue's rant
extending a radio arm to grab one listener and shake her
a lightning-wristed fist to punch another in the face

Laughter fear gluttony tenderness ambition curiosity
all these profitable signals over the public air waves
leased to Broadcasting Corporations with patriotic names
American Columbia National tall and imposing as
the gray rib fortress towers of WPA Federal Buildings
air waves meaning frequencies peak to sinoid peak
in the oscillator the bright serpent without end undulating
waves in the ether bearing words notes and sound effects
scattering into it like bright tiny drops of information

No matter that Einstein Bohr and Heisenberg explained
why there was no ether after all for the ripply waves
to travel through instead waves of likeliness and
unlikeliness entered the Philco and Electrolux boxes
in stiff living rooms and steamy kitchens where only
humans were animate their ears tuned to speaker buzz

Out of the boxes with their dials and flickering lights
emerged actual air waves waves of sound mysteriously
turned by vibrating grains of carbon in the diaphragms
into electrons flowing down a wire then transformed

by glowing diodes full of nothingness countless
little glass Saracen helmets for incandescent ghosts
uttering air waves that are waves not of air but
of "Newton's particles of light" passing invisibly
through walls and bodies bringing their own news

For Newton's particles radiant unseen are Einstein's
immortal and fungible photons the reserve currency
of the universe the original waves from fourteen
billion years ago always waving goodbye No matter
how fast we are moving seeing thinking or talking
the air waves are faster faster than the announcer
spieling soap motor-oil borax empire and of course
radios The air waves of swing bands Father Coughlin
and FDR the Blues the Shadow and the Grand Ole Opry
waves of poverty-pain music and fantasy revenge
waves of rhetorical breath and sentimental harmony

Speaker pressure waves pressed the brains of listeners
into brain waves the wingèd word riding the wavèd air
that is not air that is not even emptiness that is doubt
Yet the certainty of "American" and Jesus and C Major
still today rides waves of uncertainty as the photons
move through every possible path to their destinations
their paths described in twiggy diagrams of QED
branching across an infinite number of universes
but always choosing the precise instant we inhabit
On the Air cramped and padded studios oak podiums
with diamond and club and spade shaped microphones
floated on curving air on its waves an invisible ocean
whose ripple-reflective surface is the ionosphere
Signals leapt up from it like flying fish to the stars
or in shoals darted down to the other side of the world
Short waves made waves in crystals that feed earphones
from kit radios amid Popular Science and baseball cards
Spanish Hindi Afrikaans in each boy's night skull

Cryptic voices surged and crisscrossed on static swish
airless air waves whose ripples radiate weaker and
weaker out into the black vacuum of the cosmos

Today's air waves are full of conversations text images
messages thought to be private phone to tiny phone ring
tones like raindrop rings on pond after pond after pond
connected delivered replicated and reproduced by
towers satellites negotiating passing on the signals
in ripples of zeros and ones   The electrons now racing
through logic gates in conduits too small to reflect
light as anything but a noise cloud of broken waves
take every possible path to their destinations
and each bit the gate measures defines our universe

So a woman's voice hoarse with exhaustion and longing
arrives in my ear from the far departure gate through which
she will depart for here after so many hours   There snow
observed by light from the big night window flickers
into existence descending like silent static on wind waves
and is gone as her cracked sweet whisper of my name
falls through me air waves to waves of wanting synapse
It's the coming collapse of the wave function into a single
solution her arrival soon from the other side of the air
setting her bags down as she leans into my arms

Dark Energy

Black inhuman plumes of entropy ascend from bombed Iraq wells and exploded tanker cars in Quebec

Great black snake sways its many-eyed head as it tries to find a way south from boreal tar desolation past Lakota drum-shields

Black coal soot coating the earth's lungs paling to ghost-gray and pink coughing froth as all Beijing becomes a forbidden city

Capital intelligent black cancer swirling in the eyes of executives commands them to create Venus climate in the skies of Gaia

Blackness invisible in well-lit rooms and cubicles rises through the floors to form face-eating mirrors like liquid obsidian

Despair transmutes to viridian light in alembic hearts as voice-crowds face down the black uniforms of planetwide extinction

Energy of convection flows between black outer robe and white inner robe of a Bedu woman soaked in sun

DMV

Backs to the wall are two
                         lines of black plastic chairs
                                               wavering rippling but nearly
stationary like a score
                         composed of seated bodies, pairs
                                               or triplets leaning their heads
together to murmur, or
                         isolates leaning forward fingering
                                             tiny screens or a book's pages
The score changes slowly
                         as some stand and shuffle to a gap
                                             in the glass partition under
a black number where
                         a blank clerk waits while the system's
                                           mechanical angel chants
Now serving [alphanumeric]
                         at Window number [digits] as if
                                         opening a gate of flowers
for each ticket holder who
                         will arrive clutching the filled-out
                                         forms plastic card or cash
Many are here to gain
                         or regain their encoded transactional
                                       selfhood, their permission
to pilot a private steel capsule
                         through flat spacetimes highly
                                       regulated yet competitive

dull yet murderous, where dark

        energy flows from proximity

                to expand phobic distance

To be close is to be at risk

        Every other-driver head is a

                singularity a facebox whose

decision outputs beyond

        the event horizon of metal and tinted

                glass must be predicted

Here heads and their bodies

        work-tired or workless in drab jeans

                windbreakers, tights, line

up as if at lights or signs

        or simply at clogs or stoppages in

                the multichannel network

that moves each one like

        a data packet among earn-state

                pay-state and rest-state

Heads and their bodies their

        faces so many shades of brown

                tan, amber, pale, all view

the same promises rescinded

        options foreclosed into decaying

                orbits of roads and days

Which is why some now forced

        to idle in administrative traffic

                on their way to a window

turn to face each other

        through stranger-space as if through

                lane-space, stepping invisibly

out of their stalled vehicles
                   of personal necessity: some
                                        still sleek, some battered, but all
engineered like make and model
                   around different price points
                                        around different income
gender, education, skin
                   tone, data points connectable
                                        through the alphanumerics
on each license into n-dimensional
                   dummies of 0s and 1s designed
                                      to define them   They
now talking joking raise
                   a tiny Commons like a scarlet tent
                                      on Identity's factory floor

Philosophical Panorama

for Guillermo del Toro

At sunset the line of hills undulates like a lazy signal in the infra-red
and behind them curtain behind gray curtain paling the mountains
cordilleras fluttering with infinite slowness in the geological wind
like worn muslin the strata exposed and angled near vertical
a decor of ghosts the ancient shells hanging in the tatter and weave

Even the sky is veined and streaked with evening like weathered wood
as if the entire landscape were facing you inside a vast open crate
Atop weathered wooden tables nearer at hand conclusions are displayed
in uneven rows cardinal red and white folded around each other
furled like flayed pig-ears or artificial damask roses of painted steel

Twelve ponderous men in black suits are reaching the tables now
in an uneven file They do not wish to be walking in step yet they are
They stride up one at a time to inspect these results their square faces
pale as flyleaves in the volumes of old leather-bound monographs
their certitudes protruding from their taut jaws like black cheroots

Behind the men and the white village the line of the hills darkens
the slow massed whispers of the indeterminate woods advancing
down into the valley as twilight deepens and shaggy clouds converge
yellow-eyed with innumerable paired fire-balloon lanterns hovering
as if they scented the intellectual blood about to be spilt below

Each man takes a conclusion to press to his muscular well-fed chest
Tongue-like blades and articulate rods glide out of its little sliding doors
and dart between the man's ribs under his formal suit and shirt
Swiftly the conclusions rearrange the internal workings of the men
into logics that feed themselves like Klein bottles carved of muscle

Vertiginous gulfs in the men's interiors open and inhale like sea-caves
so that the idiot village of white blocks is hypnotized by this emptiness
the houses cubical with black iron trellises and brackets holding impacts
where unbearable wishes have struck the layered belief structures
blood geraniums and poppies decorating blank black-windowed walls

All the windows are open on evening and the women look out
from rooms where they have been preparing the dream-sleep of Reason
hair streaming down their backs then lifted by the tectonic breeze
like hydrographic maps of underground streams in the limestone twilight
They cease their contemplation of oneiric objects and turn toward you

Silent wide-eyed the women watch you and the men who stand swaying
like poplars like demons in the fiery uprushing music of their involution
as they lift the bloodstained conclusions to their lips and kiss them
before collapsing in on themselves folding to red origami and vanishing
leaving behind the formal syllogisms of their empty suits and shirts

Now Doubt lifts a colorless arch over the village like ice around the moon
Before dawn it will be overgrown with vines from the split conclusions
and under it the children will dance awkwardly in their nightgowns
until the white cottages are tossed in the huge hand of night like dice
and thrown down onto the gray-grained weathered wood of this world

The children lead their mothers and grandmothers from the cottages
out into suspension of belief and disbelief where your contradictions
ripple and fold into each other as cloud layers and mountain strata fuse
where beyond them the sun is about to split open like a pomegranate
forescattering the trillion incandescent crimson tears of probability

Painscape

for Etel Adnan

Larvae of lightning nibble and crawl inside the sagging clouds.
No rain, only heavy mist that blurs outlines into mercury beads.
Buildings, vague, loom up, vanish, seem to switch neighborhoods—

Narrow blank houses with steep roofs and spiked iron railings,
Machine shops where drills screech, or presses irregularly slam,
Office towers of stained roughcast concrete, glare-ceiling stores.

In the cathedral, behind grey-yellow brick, thin off-key singing;
Statuettes of the Hanging God wear crown-ribbons of black drip,
Their eyes fixed wide-open upward like a rabbit's at spine-snap.

Trees, varicose and leafless, spread slick twigs along the streets
Above passers-by: tight-lipped women, men with thick necks
And small eyes, children screaming, yanking repeatedly slapward.

In the houses, on fling-crumpled beds and warping upright chairs,
Under the scratch and pinch of clothing or exhaustedly naked,
Flesh smears as dread tunnels within it, as the brain bruises itself

By attacking the skull, as faces puff out and collapse in the wind
Of stunned conversations that finish in mid-sentence or a punch.
After dark, traffic is arthropods—cat-size centipedes, spider-crabs

And little oily-backed scuttlers, mouth-parts moving elaborately.
Claws dance in vertebral ripples of scrape over garbagey asphalt.
From all around, the intermittent, unmerciful shattering of glass.

Salton City

Our day-strata: first, desert horizontal, Highway 86 beveling the sand horizon
where semis glide by both ways 24/7 trailing hollow spumes of white noise,
long data blocks led by their tractor tags to be decompiled in some terminal.

Above them fade the mountains: bare rock, lavender, taupe shade, fractal crags
on the far side of the Sea's cerulean line holding the sky in a lithium mirror
as it shrinks within an ever-wider border of bleached fish skeletons and sand.

And nearest, the labyrinth of pothook streets named for long-ago astronauts
or makes of car, as if the future was already over: rows of ranch-style stuccos
trailing off like senile sentences into creosote, tumbleweed, or barren gravel

where concrete caps for water and power hookups are still nestled under scrub,
fossil trilobites of a double evaporation: home values and blue-glass water
as the State hesitates to filter the Sea's salts and re-flood it with a Mexican river.

But the neat beige houses built for snowbirds pump out norteñas and Mexi-pop
now, men cluster round an open hood or in folding chairs watching TV soccer
as their kids hummock ATVs along dry washes that go all the way to the skyline.

Then at night the autumn stars ascend in their orders, Orion leading his white dog
under the arching Vía Láctea, the galaxy's edge, spiraled with habitable planets.
The Sea goes on shrinking but a river, sinewy and brown, is already flowing north.

The Season

No longer the Salton Sea
with its necklace of fishbones and collapsed marinas
guano spatter   reeds   algae stink
it's the desert they want

Huge mobile homes and RVs
painted in flaring stripes and swirls
stream
one after another
south on the 86
race bikes racked in back   jeeps in tow
pull in at Arco AM-PM oasis
tacos bottled water beer cigarettes ice fuel
right turn   out along the Salton Seaway
corrugated into asphalt waves
they   ride   like   ships
headed away
from the Sea

Gather on bare flats   backdrop a looming arc
of stark gray-pink scree slope mountains runneled
by gone rain
scrub-dotted in slate twilight   Assemble
temporary suburbs   wheeled oblong bungalows
spaced   well   apart
just like home
faraway burr of diesel generators
blue propane stars under grills
lawn chairs   chilled six-packs

Anza-Borrego Desert State Park
where they park

sedimentary layers   buff   taupe   faded rose
ancient Pacific floor
tectonic uptilted   then weather-planed off
under traveling cloud shadow
winding canyons and arroyos
ghost rivers where water once found ways
no flow in years
but wind

Now ORVs and dirt bikes buzz and snarl along them
swarming metal insects
eat the dry
Martian silence
piloted by boys in helmets visors masks
tight coveralls
patterned with death's-heads or flames
so many
fine dust plumes rise   merge into   beige haze
under pale blue winter vault

their other plumes invisible
combusted
clear   refined   aromatic
hydrocarbons
not just the engines   theirs and parents'
24/7 A/C   fridges   lights

while the young riders faceless in their spaceman gear
veer bouncing along washes
track ruts between   sandstone hill hummocks
low mesas
like those desert kingdom princelings
carefully taught
never to pick up what they drop

After they pass
scatter crows return   as silhouettes on ridges
quick rabbits   re-emerge to nibble
coyotes   nosing   resume the hunt
the vague dust   slowly
settles
the carbon
keeps going
the desert forgives   it is made   of abraded time
the   climate
not

Geysir

Under far
cumulus cliffs
in a circle
of bone soil
one vapor plume
leans and twists
Brief white spurts tease
with collapse
until ghosts boil
ascending
peaked hoods and
shoulders warp up
a scroll with
winter mountains
become flame-
tongues of wild steam
Rock fissures
over magma
shout old rain
back at heaven

Old Faithful, Yellowstone National Park, October 2012

What the Rain Said

After so long dry
after fire-floods
washing forests to ash
erasing Paradise
this numberless choral
whisper of blessing
after so long unheard
the language foreign
but familiar

the sound myriad
momentary fingers
delicately but
persistently
touching the earth
a grandmother's
withered cheek
asking, asking
Are you okay?

Then as I drive
under pigeon grey
sky over hiss
of wet desert dust
in the wheeled herd
pumping yet more
burnt breath
into saturated air
slaps and
slaps my glass
face: *Fool!*

Across the highway
in shallow dips

runoff makes mirrors
in which we still
don't see ourselves
our scorched
diminishing leafage
of futures
our twelve years left
only pouring sky
a false forever

Outside now
as I gaze up
my own eyes wet
with the unspeakable
question I
speak in silence:
Ancient always
new giver
How many more
times will you
return to us?

Far off under
traveling clouds
in the cities
the crowding young
with their sun banners
crest the avenues
To them storm
reiterates the signal
given the tough
dryland seeds:
Now
Grow now!

TRIPTYCH I:
THREE SURREALIST WOMEN

Hommages to
Kay Sage, Leonora Carrington, and Remedios Varo

Egg-Head: Portrait in a Landscape

for Kay Sage

The egg-head wanders his white unfinished mansion amid broken furniture
part-covered He too is shrouded in a dust-sheet like a cape of longing
The mansion must always be unfinished under construction though silent

built without a plan staircases leading to blank walls or doors into space
cantilevered decks and causeways unrailed between high empty turrets
libraries without doors whose every volume is a window onto pale sky

printed with cloudlight in an unknown script anyway too faint to decipher
In the vaulted hall with its chessboard tiles the ghost-women in their robes
glide ceremoniously yet sensually in their endless move and countermove

fluid white samite draping their heads their invisible hips and shoulders
So many ghosts now the egg-head has lost count yet the game goes on
Beneath his dust-sheet a dense echo of the spectral drapery the egg-head

rides a body assembled from ball-jointed rods like a lay-figure's limbs
his ribs and pelvis aluminum struts and sections from dismantled bombers
The afterlight of Tokyo and Dresden phosphorus glows through his skull

He looks out over the endless plain of the everyday to the burnt horizon
the retinal scorch of napalm and the green heat-image of Baghdad burning
the world's windows fused to a shallow lake of irradiated glass in the desert

holding the chalky clouds like fossil fish in its dish of melted and fused time
beyond the walls of the egg-head's immense white wayward cubist fortress
The egg-head's face if he has one at all is concealed by his elaborate mask

The mask a streamlined curvilinear skull-cage of steel strips and bolts
holds a swiveling array of lenses that he continually shifts across his gaze:
lenses that magnify traces of infamy, lenses that focus the Empyrean blaze

between world's end and God, lenses that show money's veins and arteries
or display numbers the blood of the universe streaming in the firmament
lenses that capture the enigmatic gestures of the wind among the towers

The entire teeming city of noises and smells and quick body-traffic beyond
has seemingly vanished leaving only skyscrapers of scaffolding ascending
from the smog each one containing the mummy of an angel wound in canvas

He stares out across the invisible city full of people he cannot hear or touch
Jeweler's loupes telescopes interferometers magnetic imagers heat sensors
rotate on their geared arms across the hidden places where his eyes must be

The motion grinds at his head in its cage driving perspectives like spikes
into his brain behind the swooping intersecting metal ribs across his face
his hair rising from his head like dead grass from a boulder wound in wire

The egg-head turns from the city's unreachable crowds and the vacant air
He walks clicking along colonnades back to his study a half-finished heaven
The lenses are filling his brain's coiled glass nautilus cells with clear gel

Soon despite the complex windings and attachments round his smooth skull
its top will split open and enormous dragonflies like double-barred ankhs
haloed with vision will climb precisely out over shattered glass and bone and

veer away Their clear-vein wings waking a map abandoned by its maker
they zoom over women who at long last revealing human faces can saunter
with unraveled grace down streets leafing into voice under a green sky

In the Center of the Forest: A Topology

for Leonora Carrington

In the center of the forest underlit with winter a girl in a red cape rides
her thick dark hair billowing smoke from her brain's glowing furnace
Her cape floats and flaps behind her like the bloody flag of the moon
which has just risen over the trees a chariot wheel of pale Gaelic gold
twin to the living wheel of wood she rides along the frost-crackled path
Green mantis twigs are sprouting from each end of its miraculous axle
on which she braces her pale callused feet as if in stirrups as it rolls
She is going to visit her Wolf-Grandmother with a basket of fresh eyes

In the center of each eye is reflected the same town an adobe labyrinth
its walls in the moonlight inviting as pages whose trapdoor windows
open letting the reader plummet into abandoned chambers of childhood
Pheasants with trailing feathers intricately arabesqued in shades of black
wander the streets lined with leafless trees their branches night's arteries
The girl in the red cape rides her rumbling wheel between she-centaurs
They are cantering over spark-struck cobbles clenched like stone fists
yet arranged in spirals of occult calligraphy to be translated by the stars

In the center of one cobblestone is a vast estate hidden by high walls
Its courtyards patios and colonnades are home to anomalous animals
Antelope-men dance in a slow line their horns uncoiling like heredity
Ferret-girls glide undulant and sly down geometric rows of orange trees
Jackal brides masked in their white gowns descend moss-grown stairs
one at a time into cold lunar glare as the minotaurs they are to marry
look on admiringly their heavy chests pressing out black evening coats
All fall silent as the red-hood girl rides past her dark nebula streaming

In the center of the great hidden demesne is a mansion of many mansions
a chateau of axioms where philosophers gather to experiment and dispute
They stoop in black gowns elderly fetuses their bald white heads bulging
over faces pinched from dividing the cosmos into squares of brazen wire
Their chambers are stratified with books whose pages open like windows
of houses in moonlight allowing their characters to flutter out escaping

from the scrutiny of the scribes becoming blackbirds with red illumination
under their wings as they flock round the scarlet cape of the wheeling girl

In the center of one page in one fallen book is pictured a kitchen its vault
hung with retorts and alembics as well as iron pans pots and implements
And in carved cabinets are countless vessels filled with captured sound
the sound of an entire ocean its waves hissing and shattering malachite
shoulders against cliffs overhung like dogma the sound of a thin tempest
whining among the broken towers of cities on Mars two billion years ago
the sounds of goatskin drums and bare feet stamping all night round a fire
and now the sound of a racing wooden wheel and a girl astride it singing

In the center of the kitchen is a long plain table many women crowd around
some elderly hooded their lips like narrow canoes becalmed in sea-wrinkles
Their gaze pierces the stained muslin of the mundane to see the others even
more ancient yet youthful the ladies of the Sidhe pale nude and translucent
Their lungs patterned like damask wings of moths are visible in their chests
on either side of their hearts whose valves are doors open on a scarlet cave
arched like the hood of a cape surrounding a girl's face and smoke-coil hair
or a red lily's throat or a napkin corner-lifted over a basket of blonde eyes

In the center of the cave young women graceful in their robes as madonnas
but with hair cropped like manes bristling back from white elegant skulls
move about the immense vaulted room tending the snaky fire in the grate
feeding homunculi teaching mandrakes to sing past their cloven tongues
Seated to one side Her face a lovely sail of skin stretched between Her horns
is the Magna to the other side Wolf-Grandmother smiling with sharp teeth
Below her lace cap and veiled eyes the soft gray fur whitens round her lips
as she awaits the girl her inheritress who is bringing her the fruit of sight

In the center of the table amid lamps of red wine clusters of black grapes
is a great luminous egg orbited by dragonflies like blue comets   Inside it
the glass form of a swan-bottle whose long neck curves back into its breast
Now down the stone flags of the corridor comes a rumbling like the herds
of Popocatépetl as the girl in the cape arrives her black hair-smoke rising
The women pluck up the eyes irised green and gold she spills on the table
in time to see the great egg not breaking unfolding into a vast white rose
In the center of the rose is a forest its leaves bloodlit by the summer moon

The Sphere of the Nephilim:
A Cosmography for Two Voices

for Remedios Varo

In the sphere of the Nephilim are no fields only forests
The sphere of the Nephilim is a world greater than ours
move and live on its inner surface the antipodes lost
heavens

no roads it is always autumn
but inside out so all things
on the far side of the

The dun sky continually weaves and branches itself
which are the intricate equations of entropy spreading
a neural cascade rising from trees through thick dusk

out of fall's twigs and moss
like a pattern of fine cracks
in this unending twilight

Under the sky-forest shade whether in solitary towers
wander the Nephilim somber slender and colorless
as a cat's or a mantid's above long-limbed elegant forms

or in narrow lamplit streets
their faces tapered triangular
Half-angel mutants aware

of their incompleteness their wings absent but implied
They ache for great nebular pinions folded or outspread
they do not want them gazing out of pale beautiful eyes

in the set of their shoulders
but must always pretend
with the sadness of captives

As if to console them the sphere cares for them all
in high-walled gardens and lanes where they like to live
ancient as if the windows had looked out on centuries
them

extruding red stone houses
uplifting tall cities already
The sphere tries to dress

raising the floor's perspective to drape their bodies
of their frock-coats choristers' robes or evening gowns
forgotten
the graceful pale half-luminescent bodies they wear

when they grow too weary
The Nephilim have

are after all hybrid machines

composed of more of countless tiny Turing machines
The sphere is their terrarium their womb their nest
to closeness and the bettering of their minds and eyes

reading ribbons of wet silk
where they apply themselves
seeking whatever way out

The Nephilot women hear starlight as lines of music
or to embroidering the slow flow of the sphere's fabric
Their thick fair hair is alive and though always worn in

They attend to playing
out of their fingers unfurling
closed wings on their heads

can spread into moonbursts or red chameleon tongues
that wander the finely fibrous clouds of interior sky
to turn wheels and belts that spin music into white grids

The males of the Nephilim cosmologists or detectives
dissecting clocks dismantling the abacus of harmony
crush
from siphoned moss-nebulae a phosphorescent elixir

but must feed instead to the crescent moons that breed
segments of pearly lemon become philosophical heads
as a few also would snare women within whose bodies

Some Nephilim aware their sky is a mere cloud-trap
succumb to melancholy and melt into their furniture
or owls forgetting their confinement by the great sphere

they hunt birds or invisible mice in the overgrown grass
the Nephilim must keep traveling the men mostly alone
Both ride unicycles their long tracks like the grooves

cogged wheels on the inner surface of a big brass globe
of symbolic planets and stars arrayed on shining rods
universe below beyond their always spinning spokes

Some venture on water onto clear tessellated waves
whirlpools
tiered holes through the sea's vitrines into a green
like Dante's of paradise the helical ascending gardens

these wise Nephilim believe they must climb to escape
Pedaling single-wheel paddle-boats with eggshell hulls
to Spiral City with its one canal incurving to the center

the crested four-winged Swift Woman stirs restlessly
the single passenger she will bear to the sky's interior
having seen the pilgrim caught in the radiant millwork

to seize on the tiny planets
and whose rotation they use
they wear as seclusion

investigate time and space
With other engines they

they are forbidden to drink

in the center of their sphere
they cage for questioning
are chimeric windows

between earth and earth
Others revert to cats
in the small sphere of Now

But to avoid these fates
the women in close troupes
curving and looping of

controlling the dances
an astrolabe of the invisible
they assume is boundless

avoiding the slow

circled inferno the inverse
a bright nautilus tower

their vast mundane shell
they make pilgrimage
There in a sandstone belfry

on her perch awaiting
She will return in silence
of the event horizon

ringing the black singularity at the center of the sphere
and instantly flattened a tape charged with instructions
as all the information coded in his hair eyes and brain

The ancient sphere does all it can to prevent such losses
after slow turning years to the same point they are made
legs now mere forks for the full circle of iron extruded

in surrender to endless gyring round their hollow world
along the paths of the forest cyclists of metamorphosis
the wheel spinning beneath the body's vertical hour-hand

When Nephilot women halt like automata whose tape of
the sphere absorbs the smooth brittle shells of their bodies
in the walls of old houses as knowledge phantoms gazing

Mute as Piero de la Francesca seraphs in understanding
like layered leafy vulvas they have grown in the plaster
to show the narrow-gazing men what they have learned

into new translucent but multiversal bodies of knowledge
in which as they now see the reflected crescent moon
of the one in the interior night thick with decision twigs

They perceive they were not angels' crippled offspring
So a last vortex opens whirling apples and pomegranates
as each newly self-scripted one dives from her own sex

the pilgrim's form stretched
unreeling into the dark
falls out of the cosmos

When Nephilim return
less human but less angel
from their delicate bones

They start rolling again
balanced on perpetual motion
set always at midnight

desire commands has run out
but pupates their minds
back like trapped reflections

they reach urgently from slits
gesturing pointing trying
until they will the wall's code

and step out to grasp the cup
is an exact compressed copy
storing the same written light

but their long larval stage
above the circular table
through the time-wind's eye

Triptych II: Arbor

Immigrants: Eucalyptus

Who airward lean straight, who bonetune cluster anywhere
who always infringing, who grey scrawl peel to ghost-rose
who spread and flaunt seethe tents above tatters

who remember motion and moon, tide-wide arriving
who fed koala, dark-lanterned with crows in the dry stars
who knew sand, who muttered pattern-crack creeks until they ran

who writhe skin characters downstroked in rain joy
who revel pale-jade cricket shade among these thicker greens
who winter rattle shards half off at crystal angles

who sun-scatter over us, who million-talon light into seafloor
who afternoon arcades name ocean as wish
who airswimmers gather summer oils, who flare in Santa Anas

who like other raggedy comers brought for crops assessed useless
who cross equator fireweed tree, who named invader
who infill and prosper, teach here hills a near-aspen speech

who blood-orange stumps gape along the truck ruts
who lopped, who backhoed up, who trunks chaindragged in stacks
who shreds and twigs roadway litter like refugee trails

who buttons dropped wait wheel-driven under mud
who sapling asylum inside live-oak maze, on maple steeps
who unerase, who flayed under crescent crowns keep rise

Mask Forest: Madrone

Lean half-sleek trunks
        hot copper streaked with ocher
                intertilt and fork between
here and there growing near
        through each other over y to
                x in a ravine roof arch
black knobs blank like night-
        eyes in the smooth undermasks
                where low twigs were
though oval leaves ray-blade
        green from gold flare layer
                among outveining boughs
Bark square-end scales
        like dragon-hide curl blacken
                peel up in plane shavings
They unmask thorn-vine
        scars rising in a coil the tree's
                own world-line about sun
or show a grain of deep
        red meat-scores flowing around
                stumps like a blood river
Others are ridged and webbed
        with crisscross wrinkles fine as
                on the back of my old hand
Wood newly bared orange
        and green-bronze then rose-
                tangerine pales to puce ember

remasking after rain-rub

        smooth as young flesh when

                Apollo flickered girl to tree

half-nude in swirl bark

        tatterflakes below stalled upward

                reach of her pleading arms

Now soil-sunk groins

        of roots heap a lumpscape whose

                gnarl and grip moss furs

tonguing and fronding out

        same tendrils as millions of gone

                years toward thin grass

where blue-quartz dragonflies

        are skating over feathered

                tips in shade ground air

Shadow Rhapsode: Apple

In wind is this flicker-country, is fret screen woken to afternoon
where you, apple tree, wave in shadow narrows between houses…
In wind, in westlight your mottle on wall upshifts to opposite forest,

it unblurs in a sparrow motion, mimicking flutter-down or settle
to quick pecks and adjust, sidestep, shakeout of feathers in focus—
In wind you pendulum stem-spiders, dark hooks, rearback scuttle

down on wing shivers in the tangle, or dry-mandible each other—
In wind your shade-jungle diagonals, of stalky eaters, of tooth-leaf
leaning peer over trail, draw small peddler hero flailing in his climb

to the dance gardens, veil-tremble overhung with nods and kisses
In wind you dangle a puppet battle, filigree soldiers in spine-gear,
in dragonfly capes, lean side for parry and stab, twist or fall still,

In wind your quickness palace, awake statues and eye-move hidden
by alcove, by curtains restless up conjuror stairs, by sudden stars—
In wind is your semaphore, your flat-array-only fruit of motion

takes up shit-mutter, stiff day-nod between these us non-neighbors,
you turn all to air theater, hung gamelan of whisper-discs all angles,
In wind your shake-web of thought, story leaves loose to meeting.

Branchings

Branchings

for Bonnie Murray Tamblyn

Poplars

From the below-stairs lavatory off the front hall
narrow window at ground level
view of ranked poplars interspersing beech hedge
across the gravel yard, wide-reaching roots so thirsty
they had pulled down half the old front of the house
when my father was a boy
green shifty and murmuring in wet spring winds
in autumn leaves yellow carpeting the drive
part of the tessellated floor under our apple trees
On the bookshelf in that white-plastered cave
The Voyage of the H.M.S. Beagle Around the World
At five, voracious, I began in the middle:
the coast of Chile
huge fossil megatherium bones
exposed in the cliffside…
I bore the gold-edged vellum thickness of pages
held in their jewel-box of Victorian binding
up into the sitting room and asked my question
On the back of an unpaid bill my father drew me
our branch of the family tree
the writer, he said, was my *great-great-grandfather*
Already an incomprehensible weight of *greats*
began to settle on my bony little shoulders
but I felt there too the shadow-roots of wings
The weight grew as I grew, I crossed an ocean and a continent
to shake it loose and walk in my own light
Between my scapulae
the wing-roots waited

Redwoods

On old Cowell Ranch land
Santa Cruz Mountain foothills
above the new campus, fresh gray concrete, stucco, red tile
the vast, sweet silence of sequoia woods enduring
soft dark-rose bark in needle-filtered light
converse of jays and finches high out of view
the openings between the redwoods' far-off summits
ridge-top caves in the sky
Silent under their colonnades
looking downslope seaward alone
or with new friends almost as dumbfounded as I was
by their immensity
I dreamed the forest's ancient old-growth ancestors
from the late Jurassic
great yards-thick shade pillars widening their dark-green myriad
embrace of the same descending fog
between them dinosaurs ponderous or quick
stalking and stamping over this recently upraised seafloor
already layered with russet duff, soft
as fine-woven rugs
decaying slowly into black humus by "the action of worms"
floor of an imagined
ocean of time
four billion years deep
my own ancestor taught us how to navigate
and sound

Pines

Hiking with housemates above the Little Sur River
sophomore year, May 1970
Across the Pacific bombs were plummeting down
60,000 pounds of payload per 159-foot-long
B-52 Stratofortress per drop
in precise arrays on towns and temples
raising blast-fountains
of wood, stone, soil, blood, bone
while we strode up the coastal trails hefting
frame-packs and rolled mummy-bags
aluminum cups hooked on our belts
for dipping the cool, still-safe creek water—
Long-legged, wide-lunged
I came up a ridge-side trail ahead of the others
out of shaggy stands of knobcone, bristlecone, Ponderosa
and a few Monterey, not yet flesh-eaten by bark beetle
breathing green-gold new summer
air between their verticals
cones everywhere like fallen lanterns
faint watersound mingling
with breeze whisper through the tapered crowns
Looked out from the ridge spine
between lichened live-oaks and crimson-skinned madrone
To one side: forest riding the crumpled coastal hills
pushed up by crust collision
to the other: silver-white fog
breeze-rippled roof over the near Pacific
No sign of human presence, human use
The great invisible doors of wilderness opened
on a world without us

Elms

Everywhere on drained former fenland
now fields of wheat and barley
around my first home
stands of old elms, some a hundred feet high
narrow and dark-skinned, lower trunks
thick with glossy ivy,
branches beginning always too high to climb
where rookeries made cacophonic music
clouds of the big black birds below colorless sky
would rise and scatter as I passed beneath
to play in wet weeds by the drainage ponds with their sunken
boughs looming under black water
Trees my father drew in pencil and charcoal
with exquisite precision
along with oak and beech and the glimmer
of their reflections in ponds and slow-moving streams
When I returned as a grown man
we walked in the autumn fields
of my childhood
under the same neutral sky between beech hedges
across rain-wet fallow acreage, all the elms
gone
tarred stumps where the cloud-reaching trunks
had rotted from imported sickness and been sawn down
empty spaces left behind
like gaps in a family album
or the gaps widening in my dying mother's brain
So he gestured toward those tall absences rookless and silent
with no speech but an indrawn breath
and the tears in his eyes

Aspens

1.
October in the year in this still-new century
and in the long year of my life
We drive up the 385 into the Sierras
through Red Rock Valley, scarps exposing
upthrust sedimentary layers
crimson with iron and everywhere jumbled
stacks and cairns of black fire-boulders, litter
of ancient explosions
Then above 7,000 feet the turnoff
in drizzly twilight
where June Lake opens like an eye
gazing back at a Hunter's Moon
In the morning the aspens crowding around town
whisper their thousands of yellow secrets
revealed in rising wind
from under their summer green, spreading them
for anyone to read who can
as the poplars did for me
like pages of books I might have written
drawings my father did not have time to make
and Charles wrote in shy defiance, closing
his brief Autobiography
I have therefore nothing to record during the rest of my life,
except the publication of my several books
yet in his notebook a year after his voyage ended
he had sketched a new Tree of Life
whose roots are still cracking and uptilting
ancient continents

2.

I would bring him here, my ancestor
to this still uninterrupted
unbranded landscape, inviting him
to step out of his life-size marble statue where he sits
by the great staircase
in the London Museum of Natural History
walk forward across 150 years
thousands of miles to a mountain autumn
I cannot be his eyes
that made out the branching shapes of the Great Barrier Reef
before seamen had mapped it
nor his son Francis' eyes,
father's grandfather, lover of leaves and stems
who diagrammed peering through his brass microscope
viridian machineries of photosynthesis
nor my father's
who recorded so tenderly
bark's delicate signatures and shifting ensembles of foliage
But let them all be here with me
to my shoulders no longer weight but lift
helping me open and spread wide
my own perception
surrounded by these aspens a community
whose discourses travel below soil
through shared root systems
as they shed their vivid leaves
in preparation for the coming necessary cold
before the turning
of another year

October 2016

Daimones

The Anniversary

In your recession I like a maple shake shadow, I lose by sidelong;
In the flat year's thinning of us, in this terse fade you've wagered,
In the no-globe you've blown, widening from wires around me,
I know gone of our green-wind walk, of faceward, of uttering kiss

In our wanting letters undone, straggling as ant-lines into white
In our hear-share sloughed, our summer corridor back-slammed,
Your closure to phone bless, to sleep-charm, to woken window
Sonars a fear-turn from all's offer, from friend in lie-lash and snap

In your peeling of old self-torn, of wine-mask, our join is crumpled
Your scars pale, you heal now as who, as far: I tiny down that lens
In this numb gulf under household, under wake to the sky's hole
Inside nipped O, a fallout of light from big time, I go stop-motion—

In this one-way split, in this horizon-fall, in this mirror diminish
I-was codes into I-less, all you called out lost in the leaves' tremor

Her Hatred

Like the blades of a hallucinating knife-thrower it defines its object

It meets her on a dark street with a bouquet of white-hot wires

Its thin crimson vines loop and pry into fissures in love's bark

Until it hatches a snake with a fine-boned insinuating human head

Winding a muddy river between mirror towers of righteousness

It twists back to nip and gnaw at itself like a flea-ridden dog

It shrinks her own mouth slowly to a sad copulation of worms

A scarp of old voices it is buckled and thrust up by this collision

Where a white one-eyed judge sits inside a rose of slamming doors

As it sends ten thousand boots out onto the glass floor of Heaven

A skinless horse it gallops over unending salt-flats under noon

Sweat

for George Mattingly

In these dog-day afternoons I trickle down my-
self a tall candle in the sunshine forgetting why
it was lit and becoming a stalagmite in the blue
cave of sky a wet column of minerals contoured
by time among a forest of others But none of us
here gulping down water feeling it dilute again
the ancient ocean washing the shores of our cells
is a pillar of slow stone growing Instead it's Time
that sluices over our bodies as they stand or stride
rinsing us away while it cools flesh from the blaze
of the billion suns inside us leaving salt streaks
like trajectories of tears or August shooting stars
down the cheeks of the bodiless statues we become

The Sobs

for Shoshana Wechsler

Each a quick air-fall
                    of brightness, jerk
                                    on the ripcord
                    of a widening cry,
        undulant
                throat-scarlet silk of it,
                                    dive after
                                            dive into gusting rain,
                into the lungs' coral caverns
                                    after scalding pearls
They pass
                like cars fast on a night highway,
                                    headlights blinding—
        Yet under such dazzle
                            hammer-taps too
                                    on stone doors of tombs—
                Immured grief-mummies, their
                                shriveled eyes blind
                    to all after origin,
awake again, smoothing
                        and swelling, stretching mouths
                                        wet and breathed
                they utter their names…
                                    The stop-motion misery film runs
        backwards,
                        grown man's
                                face-crumple losing its lines,

loss-frame by loss-frame

                               all the uncried, unforgiven

tongue-humblings,

              clean stabs, rust-ragged

                      slashes,

                         all

                              the falsities,

failures, the narrow wound

                and the wide

                           undone,

back-arrowing out on the

              exhale   like a numb, embering

        burst-

          open star's collapse down

                 self shaft

  out of time

      reversed—

          Then the crushed night   weight

      flares again

        into scorch,   into flame

into bright howl, radio howl,

        give-take of sky,

                eye-searing

     single vowel

   choked aleph   shattered into !A, into *Aa*   first

             letter of the body's   alphabet

repeated

     and extended   over and

                  over   and   over…

Until the breath

          runs down,

               grief's entropy   reaching its limit,

black matter   too widely   thinly

                                  spread

    for memory

      like light

         to pass between

"There are a thousand doors to let out life"

I know death has ten thousand several doors
For men to take their exits: and 'tis found
They go on such strange geometric hinges
You may open them both ways
            —Webster, The Duchess of Malfi

1.
Already in the womb is one, the placenta's aperture
like a telescope's tiny eyepiece, just opposite
the still locked, only door into this life

2.
One in the bottom of the baby's crib, a trapdoor waiting,
one facing the car-seat where he's strapped like an astronaut

3.
They flank the toddler stiffly as her parents
in a snapshot, or loom
close behind her, twitching like angels' wings

4.
I wake inside a circle of doors
inside other circles a labyrinth whose walls are doors
a glasshenge of invisible closures
through which I routinely thread my way

5.
Each door's a shutter in a panopticon
reversed: a thousand, ten thousand million
silent prisoners watch us where we sit

6.

Here in death's many-floored headquarters
corridors lined with doors, all opening
on vague offices, which, as you step inside, become
empty elevator shafts

7.

The front door the car door the parking-lot door
the basement door the furnace door
the subway-train door the main cabin door
the shower door the clinic door the storm door the

8.

Doors like two-way full-length mirrors
in which we see our own reflection
superimposed on another silhouette
whose features, dim as through ice
almost but not quite blend with ours

9.

The door in the blade. The door in the windshield. The door in the match.
The door in the tree. The door in the half-built or half-ruined wall.
The door bright at the far end of the gun-barrel,
the door biting itself in the camera shutter. The door in the wave
and in the next wave, and the one after. The door in this one's eye,
in that one's hand, held out like poem or subpoena:

10.

The door in the bottle is dimly crouched like a jinni
or an unborn fetus, furled
like an illegible message, or intricate like a ship
carved of bone, approaching from the glass horizon. . .

11.
Doors that keep sliding swiftly by just under the surface
of the road, like car shadows,
doors blowing end over end down an alley, doors peeling off
the calendar like days in an old film,
doors marching stolidly toward us on their corners
in single file, and passing through us

12.
The doors of the vanished mosque, the shattered temple,
the church leveled to its plan: empty lot with step still mounting
to empty frame, seeded grass waving beyond

13.
I stand inside a polygon of doors
doors multiplying like facets of a composite bubble
day by day tens of hundreds of thousands of
doors gasping and bursting, shimmering
with a rainbow of greed, then gone

14.
A door suddenly opens on the bedroom ceiling
through it you see the sky falling
upwards away from you
and follow

15.
After all others, at the end of a red hallway, banging loose,
always the next door, the heart—

Coevolution

O body swayed to music, O brightening glance, How can we know the dancer from the dance?

As the flowers with the bees:
generation after generation
the social wasp slowly
growing gold fur behind her head
baskets on her legs to gather pollen
proboscis to lick up wet sugars
meanwhile the corollas elaborating
folding around each thirsty visitor
caressing her with downcurved anthers
until the bee, powdered with possibilities
returns home between aisles of giant ferns
above the meter-wide splayed footprints
of therapods below the toothy shrieks
of archeopteryx in treetops, transporting
her cargo of tiny grains and data rays
She tells as dance her way to one bloom
in the steep syntax of the sun

so our brains with symbols:
generation after generation
the primate brow tilting
upward and bulging like a bud
thick jaw receding into precision
the optic nerves reaching outward
like stamens anthered with light
above the tongue's trembling stigma
the big nodding bloom of the notochord
grows more intricately layered and folded—
blood calyx, a neural corolla opening inward
drawing new social sign-swarms that hover
and swerve articulate as their forms adapt
furred uncertainty gathering quanta of sense
to be spread over synapse cascade petals
They are dances dancing paths to each
other at the hive-door of the invisible

…L'absence de toute rose

Hearts/Corazones

for Emma Luna

The sun's heart like ours growing its own death and the death of the worlds it has gathered

William Harvey's heart a simple pump with one-way valves drawing water then oil then water again out of the stolen ground

The tree's heart rising and widening through time an allegory of the sun

No the heart is a scarlet poppy that opens and closes its petals round a calyx of bitter sleep

Shakespeare's heart a busy red tavern of voices a bare stage with two doors and spirit music

No the heart is a scarlet root whose flower the body grows to be its garden

Newton's heart a clock wound by God beating without rest an absolute motion in unbounded space

The heart of Zero like the hurricane's empty eye surrounded by violence

No the heart is a timid red octopus in the sunken wreck of the ribcage

Milton's heart a vault of burning wings a globe of Eden bright as a serpent's eye orbiting the sun

No the heart is a four-gated city receiving exhausted pilgrims dispatching them to twin cathedrals of cloud sending them forth again as saints

Rembrandt's heart a self-portrait repainted continually in entropy's impasto blurring slowly with drink and grief

The heart of a humpback whale unchanging drum under long varying song

No the heart is a haunted house its doors banging windless as the revenants glide through

Mary Shelley's heart cut like her drowned husband's from her body but then sewn into the chest of a giant the reanimated patchwork corpse of Reason

      The moon's heart a mirror of pitted ice awaiting the lovers who will melt and drink it

      No the heart is a faceless medusa that turns the body to stone when it sees its own reflection

Walt's heart the clasping and unclasping of hands in the boom and hush of the Atlantic shore

      No the heart is a blackberry hanging amid the thorny vines of its arteries

Emily's heart a locked bedroom with the windows open four velvet curtains flapping in rhythm

      The heart of a mouse tiny engine of hunger the heart of a hummingbird tiny engine of trance

      No the heart is a timer wired to the body's bomb and counting down

Marie Curie's heart a counter ticking in her chest as her brain glows through her skull to light the paneled walls of authority

      No the heart is a tremulous generator whose input is forgetting and whose output is desire

Einstein's heart a singularity growing ever more massive drawing in moonligh starlight the light over Hiroshima till it falls out of the universe

      The heart of a dragonfly hurried like a child's curiosity over a field of points and lines

      No the heart is a monk in scarlet repeating his mantra so that the world will not stammer into silence nor the stars wink out

Picasso's heart a many-angled labyrinth in the shape of a woman's brain a minotaur at the center

No the heart is a child's fort high in a tree the ladder pulled up

Turing's heart a universal machine in the blood's red circuit working ceaselessly toward the problem that will stop it

The heart of One a vertical line extending to infinity in both directions

No the heart is a fast-motion calendar shedding repeated reminders of life into imaginary wind

Schrödinger's heart a camera obscura with two apertures through which blood pulses *bright dark bright dark* each pulse opening another universe

No the heart is an eye blinking as it stares along the roads of past and future

Emma Luna's heart a pomegranate spilling the scarlet seeds of vision the clarity of stars

The galaxy's heart the heart of a Sufi dancer attractor unseen at the center of outflung arms

The sun's heart mortal yet growing heavy and red with all the elements of love

Notes

William Harvey: English physician, whose discovery of the mechanism of the circulation of the blood was inspired by seeing a water-pump with a one-way valve.

Walt: Whitman, see especially "Out of the Cradle, Endlessly Rocking."

Emily: Dickinson, spent most of the last decades of her life alone in her bedroom or in the garden of her family home.

Einstein: His theory of General Relativity both made possible the atomic bomb and predicted black holes.

Alan Turing: English mathematician, cryptographer, and theorist of artificial intelligence, showed that it cannot be predicted when a computer performing a series of algorithms within a given logical system will encounter a problem that it cannot solve within the terms of that system and will cease operation as a result.

Erwin Schrödinger: German quantum physicist, originator of the famous "cat" paradox, whereby a random quantum event determines whether a cat sealed in a box lives or dies, but is neither alive nor dead until the box is opened. This paradox is resolved if it is assumed the cat lives in one parallel universe and dies in another, just as the interference pattern of bright and dark bars caused by light passing through two narrow slits onto photographic paper is caused by the light going through one slit in one universe and the other slit in the other, the two waves interfering with each other.

Sardine Machine

for Hart Crane

They shoal in sweep formation, swarming gleam
with tail-flick wave through smooth curve like a wrist
volplaning pivots, wheels, quick tinfoil stream-
line motion shines a mirror-clouded twist;
upspiraling, the myriad uncoils wide
slowly to merge, a heartform of barbed glass
in ripple assembly, pours to hanging glide,
mingling of angles in bright matrix mass…
Then, turning, round side eyes, a chorus line
of sight, as startle vision multiplies—
Unarmed armada, designerless design
of silver seraph unison, you replicant rise
around no throne but hunger's, endless flight
breeding in tiny metonymies of light

(Monterey Bay Aquarium Kelp Forest)

Handscape

Sinewy long-fingered neither for certain man's or woman's
on the back of the right the veins are a row of nested Vs

leafless each rooted in the narrow-boned flexible wrist
on the back of the left the veins form a long-legged dancer

arms raised in fear or jubilation facing a bare bough perhaps
the two backs together an allegory of the body's winter

Above them are knuckles forever red and creased like bark
fine wrinkles go sweeping round them when the palms tense

flowing down between the fingers like the runoff of years
draining into the palms the forcelines from past intentions

where the big creases fate life marriage love are done deals
carved like Utah sandstone arroyos seen from an airliner

The fingers are graceful still but with idiot smiles at the joints
puffy as stubs of lopped-off branches on an old apple tree

the nails finely ribbed as rose glass and flecked with white
All over the backs of the fingers are tiny faint pale scars

cuts chopping wood or pushing through thorns after petals
or berries papercuts cat-scratches nicks from tools or shards

characters from a provincial language barely spoken now
faded into the thinning skinscape among clustered pores or

else petroglyphs eroding soon obliterated like the memory
of what inscribed these miniature white markers of damage

each unique like the snowflake instants every one of which
is a cosmos falling through the branches of time's nightwoods

imperishable yet to be lost like this poem that the hands now
typing conclude and the hands of all who will ever read it

Climb

I believe we had been walking in the evening forest father
as once we used to climb the pine slopes of the Haute Loire
or Cotswold beech woods in green-sunk late summer sun
We must have been walking as night slowly rose from close
to the trunks into meshed radials of branches and the path
had paled to a gray stripe veering away between banks
And who but you would be my guide in these dark woods
not in the middle of my life but in the beginning of its end
And who but you father could grip my hand and carry us
up through cooling air between foliage filters whispering
into the interstitial wind blowing from the vanishing point
at the center of the still invisible horizon so that ascended
above treetop cumulonimbus flickering with butterflies
we see tall between hills the flung-wide gates of afterlight

Transfinities: On a Theme from William Blake

for my father

Thus is the earth one infinite plane, and not as apparent
To the weak traveler confined beneath the moony shade

Who cannot see all his days and nights laid out across the hills
And valleys of spacetime like a chessboard of cloud shadows
Or like a city glittering with countless thought-constellations
With channels and meshes of lights marking his decision trees
Where incidents and opportunities keep passing by motionless
Like innumerable vehicles each with its intricate passengers
Blur-knots of myriad causation in forms of women and men
And the streamlined instincts prowl and pounce in its alleys
Turning him toward doorways he would not have chosen
Open on green speechless gardens or carnivals of sensation

The traveler's country seems frontiered by his birth and death
At east and west where silences guard circular bone gates
That open only to him, his country an archipelago of presence
Mapped on the apparent globe his footfalls roll through void
Night to night, a froth-speck in an endless ocean of darkness
Finite and corrupt yet unknowable as he seems to himself
Still, between those gates the poles of his horizoned earth
The traveler in the inverse illusion that is singular mortal form
Is never alone as he believes, though all he meets and knows
Seem to enter or leave his view like spirits through walls
Or descend soundless through the floors of their bodies

Yet each of these travels upon her own earth, no less infinite
Than his, and intersecting with his and all others at angles
Unknown to length breadth and height, so each encounter
Whether on crowded pavement or inside a bedroom's hush
Or under dusklit oaks or along a room flickering with work
Is a meeting of vastnesses greater than when galaxies collide

And each plane is a helix like the staircase Jacob saw in dream
Its steps are not hours days and years but human heartbeats
So it ascends the axis of time winding its blue expanse around
The dragon-pillar of the sun, which as it rises widens reddens
Throwing off hordes of ultraviolet leopards and X-ray tigers
Preparing in its hell-womb the serpent embryos of new worlds
That will take shape after its death about stars yet to be born
Even as it widens and darkens billowing like a scarlet poppy
Until it swallows the rusty iron spirals of Mercury and Mars
Between them his Earth-stair all ocean and air scorched away
A ladder of ghosts inside the sun's cooling temporal column
Before it collapses, a vast red tower bursting its fiery chambers

So the traveler if he could unfold the wings of his perception
Would see that he is not weak that he is one of the angelic host
Climbing that staircase of instants his body even singular mortal
A colossus of inner mountains, valleys with herds of red cattle
Crowding along its riverbeds and the shores of its vast lakes
With packs of white wolves guarding its towns and provinces
Its highways streaming with pilgrims to and from the capital city
A wonder of seven gates in groin belly breast throat and brain

As the traveler moves along the hallways and boulevards
Of his country he encounters himself at every age he will occupy
Shifting from self to self to self without interruption or knowledge
For his very space, his air, is composed of the infinite number
Of his bodies from chrysanthemum of cells in the womb-wall
By way of baby hungry-brained helpless reaching for the vertical
To boy, face ungraven, running mazes of friendship and power, to
Youth shamed or proud on his long bones, pollen-grain in desire's
Knocking waters, to grown man thickening slowing as he bears
Children and work in his arms up sleep's tunnels toward day
To grandfather withering sweet on his knees with the small ones
To chrysalis creased and spotted soon to split as his heart falters

And in his journey of eighty years he will inhabit each of them
By being each of them: numberless the flesh-images of his soul
When most shrunken a phantom in a skull-cave peering out
As he thinks at a world of opacity: oaks cars a hillside sparrows
His neighbors even his child's face even the body he calls his
All closed to his five shuttered senses Yet each of these images
He has woven in his brain from strands of light ripples of air
Into the spherical tapestry he calls Life which each night
He unpicks like Penelope holding off suitors while she awaits
The return of her beloved from the marbled grip of the sea
Sifting through the threads to make new stories new selves
Each an allegory of the terrible freedom that is his in eternity
For this beloved whose name he has forgotten is his true self
Whom he will know by the memory of the road-tree that grows
Through their house whose boughs form their marriage bed

So from each body he will travel on his journey westward
He weaves the valleys where his children rise about him
Tussocks bright with scrape-flowers and flocks of questions
Until they vanish grove by grove from his perception only
To reappear each as tall woods nearer the last lightfall
His partner like him a river of slow-altering body and face
Deep-graven in meeting's hills widening to routine shallows
For each room in each home they share is a corridor of hours
Gathering shadowbars like a train passing through a station
Furniture finely scaled with his shed skin in ceaseless autumn
Waterflowers wilting in sinks, fleeing snakes of excrement
Friends' faces recurrent as blossom or the turning of leaves
And each tree in his street its own alley of branches above
A rippling banyan wall of wood thickening year by year
Dilating its summer-eye of foliage veining gray into winter
As he does: a self-grove shaken bare by time's unreal wind
Burned in the furnaces or fallen trunks rotting under moss
At the far horizon of this country of all his nights and days

From body to body instant to instant his identity leaps, light
Flickering flowing shed by the great striding form above
For even the shadow of an angel is brighter than high noon
And the traveler's soul is no more than a cell of this brilliance
As long as he waits at the spherical wall of the five senses
Yet in him beyond the time-door that unbars between breaths
If he will see it walks the angel whole in every wordfeather
And not alone but in company with countless others climbing
As they go debating warring joyfully with blades of likeness

All this he will perceive if he stares into his body's history
Which is only an atlas of this immense rhizome of event
See how his country of experience like a spindle widens
And then slowly narrows into a long habitual flicker-tube
Until the day his time is no longer bought and his paths
Loop a wild brief rosetta like a palm tree's elliptic scales
Before the spindle narrows into a final shaky causeway
A winking arcade of medicines aflutter with white hands—
Yet between these between the shutters of his loneliness
If he will only look he will see every stone or leaf or cloud
Ablaze he will hear the voice of each unfold into a choir

For each traveler's plane exists in an infinity of variants
One for every life with that genome born of that mother
At that same point in the great sea-crystal of spacetime
Arrayed below each other at first identical in every detail
Until as you gaze with a seraph's calm and fiery eye down
Through these layers of worlds as if reading a Book of Life
In which the traveler's name is entered decillions of times
Tiny change heaping on change a photon here or there
So many worlds away from where your gaze began
You see him another man altogether, imprisoned maybe
In a flickering gray cell or lost in his own overgrown skull
Or perhaps rising on solar wings from his sleeping body
Or loved by another than any he knew in the intricate life
Whose topography you have scanned, or crushed between

Accelerated metals or stillborn or confined to his childhood's
Bright primary province by a revolt of his innocent blood—

But wherever the plane of his existence terminates as it does
In countless worlds at every instant possible from his birth
Onward, illness accident or old age each instant a last gate
Seeming to open before one myriad-strong version of him
His true and eternal body plunges down like a pearl diver
Into itself through his brain's ruins a sunken city immense
Threefold in its convolutions of streets weedy with memory

And when he grasps the pearl the zero that is origin and vertex
At once it becomes vortex as his plunge inverts it his whole
World stretched by his passage into the long shining trumpet
Held to the lips of the seraph he has again become, his eyes
Fourfold in their vision as that of light itself behold his earth
And all he knew in it Every cloud city breath kiss and atom
Rolls up again into a bright opalescent spindle a single neuron
Connected at every point to all the lives he will live has lived
As he walks winged up the highway of time with his fellows
Toward eternity of which all the universes even the angels
Themselves are but shadows and whose open door is Now

The Exquisite Corpse & The New Wine: A Theogony

The Exquisite / Corpse is stretched / out on the coral of matter / Her immense magnificent
undying / limbs asprawl
deep / asleep on ever-growing / reefs of space recreated / continually / extending back-
ward and / forward through time
The baryonic / reefs a burrowing / branching apparition swarms / with dark shoals
overgrown / with anemone / radiance
defining the fractal / shoreline infinitely / involuted / lapped / by kalpa-wide abysses
whose trailed foam / is galaxies

Yet the Exquisite Corpse / reclines / as if in a June mountain meadow / temperate enough
to shelter in its equations
the consuming glory of suns / They sprout from particular / grass to bloom and spread
their dense pollen in / turn
en / gendering storm-streamered gas / giants and around and / beyond them the plumage
of comets / which whirling long
become the / seraphic wings / of steaming seas and clouds / on the rocky spheres
ringing / the stars like swung / bells
made warm by their / hells the furnaces / of disintegrating metal / whose demons fling
ten-thousand-mile / aurora sails
beyond their atmospheres / into the solar / gales and so / voyage in slowly evaporating
great / lakes / of information

The Exquisite Corpse is / riven by the fury of / creation from the instant / of Her fall
yet graceful sleeping / profoundly
in our / rare universe our / sun-valley whose meadows are walled on all / sides by slopes
and tall cliffs / of improbability
The Exquisite / Corpse has fallen / into this valley / its implicate / order and / blossoming time
out of explosive / absence

a birth-canal like the neck / of a four-dimensional / tornado fourteen billion years /
before the moment of these / words

The Exquisite Corpse a zygote / of energy fused / with possibility grown / to a femto-
quick newborn / uncurling then

sprawling and / cooling as She falls / in every conceivable / direction / Her vast / limbs
torso / and majestic / lovely head

create the very / volumes they fill Her / countless hearts' / beats are the will / of time itself
Her breathing / the cry / of genesis

Her hydrogen / blood streams / in the firmament forming / our heavens Her / hissing
serpent / veins / permeate / all space

Her womb and Her / brain one and the same / as She dreams / the countless ordered iterations of
/ accident / that are Her / children

Her skin the ghost- / fire of / beginning visible / in all directions / from within Her / immense
outstretched and whole-broken / body

The Exquisite Corpse reclines / in this unlikely but / ever / more likely valley / of the
Polyverse / where layered fields / are fertile

Electromagnetic / breezes are shaking the nuclei / surrounded / like calyces by strong- / force
petals sending the / photons

flying from them / seeds of / eternity their speed / the measure of / time spreading / Her dream
back from the / future's end

Quarks and electrons long stems / of undersong ripple and loop in seven / tiny dimensions each /
ripple a known world

She grows in / Herself a skeleton of in / visible / forces Her bones branching / in all possible
directions like a hypertree

whose manifold / fruit are stars / Her first children / blue-white mellowing to planet-warming
gold then / vast red age:

Tree whose / undetectable soil is darkness / Its mysterious weight Her / sleep itself / holds Her /
bright eyes closed / in dream

She lies / asprawl yet more and more / threaded with singularities / bearing beauty and
terror / through Her / whole extent

beyond light's motionless / absolute / rapidity / A transdimensional nerve- / forest linking
Her body's remotest / regions

buzzes with bees / of the invisible tiny / as neutrinos huge / as seraphim skimming / Her
black / expanding / inward night

The Exquisite Corpse whose / vast / imagination incorporates all / from temporal death /
back / to birth back / to Her fall

as a continual dream in / which Her myriad / children are woken one / by one to sing
the brief anthems of their / evolution

learning Her / notes Her harmonies Their choirs / among the stars bloom / then bare ruined in
extinction but / no voice lost

singing / their histories in chords / of billions on worlds wrapped in blue / water green
methane or cracquelures / of ice

And they attend Her: whale-zeppelins listen / with stressed / crystals into the heavens
from their methane shallows

tiger-eyed octopus / artisans toil over an astrolabe of / bone among tectonic / smoke-
towers / in / rich bacterial drift

red rhizomes like / unfolded brains inch together / into prairies / of delicate calyx / eyes
across their oxide wasteland

cavernous quartz-white / labyrinths cascade / with liquid thought each epochal skull /
tilting / its radio / gaze skyward

and bipeds raise / their fragile faces / from the mirror of blood and / kisses to ask / Who
knows / them knowing themselves

All of them countless / as sunflowers turn / seeking their source and / end but rooted in / time
unable to ascend / from it

The Exquisite Corpse dreams / backward toward Her / beginning broken / images of Her
history / bursting / as white fountains
from all points / in Her expanding / form like trumpet voices / from planets born / life-
elaborated / swallowed / by bloody suns
Their shoals of / thought stream / toward Her through the quantum coral / on which Her
immense / naked loveliness / rests
even as Her / aspects well up inside / the originating minds like intellectual tears /
becoming / a river / of reflecting masks

Her dreams grow / ever richer / with mythoi mathematics / philosophies /arts / other
world-patternings of sense / most
to us unknowable / all / swimming upstream against / entropy's infra-red / current
climbing the black cliffs / of Her fall
Not only / these great creatures of symbol-/ entangled myriads but instinctual /
repertoires / wiring of notochords / tropisms
converge on Her eventual wholeness / horizon / although / the spacetime ocean / seems to spread
toward absolute / zero
For time's limit is / eternity's burning / shore / that surrounds us wherever / we are within the
immensity / of Her slumber

The Exquisite Corpse one / short sleep / past to Her / but long to us / will wake eternally
and we awake / within Her
as we have / always been: whole / in Plureality which hides in each / moment / like the
fiery / forest / in the trembling seed
The infolded / dimensions closed to / us from Her beginning / comprise the convolutions
of Her dreaming / brain the rose
of time's / nonexistent / wind compassing Her own / blossoming / from nothing and
Her extension / into graceful form

Within / these dimensions the / petal geometries / of Her / beginning tremble and hum
Her music's / infinitesimal threads
weave Her body in / every variant / allowed by the laws of Her sleep Her / very
multiplicity / a harmonic / resonance
in the widening night / ocean which seen / with the eyes of / imagination is a fruitful
valley / of vision lit / by Her beauty
From each new / waking-point radiate / intellectual roads webbing / its region like retinal
neurons into / a great city
Cities upon / thought-cities multiplying / connect across / billions of light-years under
Her body's undulant / cloudscape
where everything / possible to be / known is an image of truth / so many jostling / side
by / side in the / crowded streets

The Exquisite / Corpse composes / Herself a symphony of symphonies / from these
multitudes themselves / assembled
out of civilizations / cultures hives / jungles great flocks / of signs and integers / time-swarms
of / matings inconceivable
Tasting star-fruit refreshed / with draughts of logic / the wheeling hordes / of intellectual war
shatter / each others' / armor
deaths / within / deaths great / carpets woven of / suffering whose symmetries / we / in our
singular / form cannot perceive

Dreaming She / strides gracefully over / them toward Herselves / as toward a wild /
garden / Her skin / skeined / with galaxies
glowing new / ancient like dawn / and dusk at / once / Her lacy garment / of forces
flowing / behind / Her in self-ordering swirl
We are drawn / in Her wake we / the innumerable / requiems for Her / every limit within
the far sunken valley / of Her fall
We though scattered / like the calendar / sheets of radioactive decay of / unraveling
constants / as She utters / Her last / breath

assemble into / the long dazzling shadow She / casts from eternity / we Her / children we Her progenitors / we Her genes
we Her / retroactive / wishes we at once / the infinitesimal grapes / trampled in Her press and the tasters of Her / vintage

The Exquisite Corpse / burns / into wholeness / at the cold circumference / of spacetime that is Her / empyrean door
the fire-mirror / door in which She opens / Her eyes and sees behind Her all / that She has been / all lives / and all deaths
Her waking / body is incantation / singing and sung / by the guests / at Her festival / whose lanterns / are pendant worlds
Unbreaking / alive within every / thing ever / alive the Exquisite Corpse / has drunk / is drinking / will drink / the new wine

Afterword to "The Exquisite Corpse and the New Wine"

Many texts went into the composition of this poem, though I hope and trust that it has a life of its own beyond them. First, I acknowledge the obvious—the title. Many know the Surrealist game "Exquisite Corpse," typically played as a composite drawing of "Head, Body, and Legs" by three people, each in turn adding to the previous section, of which they have seen only a few trailing lines below the fold in the paper. But the original Surrealists were poets, not painters, and the original game was played with words, not drawing. However, the game in either form had the same purpose for Surrealists: to discover the Marvelous through what they called "objective chance"—the unexpected correlation of external and internal worlds, of physical and psychic reality. The Surrealists' procedures with chance parallel chaos theory, cellular automata, and other models in which new and unpredictable order emerges from simple elements by many iterations of constrained random processes.

This essentially evolutionary perspective is very much a part of the poem's theme: the emergence of cosmic intelligence by forms of natural selection based in the underlying (mathematical) structure of reality, in a universe in which "complexity is downhill" (Cohen and Stewart)—that is, a universe whose statistically improbable fundamental constants make it perfectly suited to evolve stars, galaxies, planets, and life. The poem suggests, following Paul Davies and Bryce DeWitt, that this evolutionary process works backward and forward in time. This is not only because ordinary quantum uncertainty extends to the past as well as the future but because the laws of physics themselves would have been "fuzzy" just after the Big Bang and so "histories" with fundamental law-sets that favor the development of observers (intelligent life) would be selected. The poem further proposes, following an idea of David Darling's, that conscious life and the universe would reciprocally create each other in a continual selection process as consciousness grew and linked up throughout spacetime via controlled singularities. Employing poetic license, I have framed the poem's opening in the organizing metaphor of Leonard Susskind's *The Cosmic Landscape*, which actually argues (following some implications of string theory) that all possible universes exist in what I have called the Polyverse. Thus, in a quantum-like way, I have "superposed" at least three cosmological explanations for the highly improbable "bio-friendliness" of the universe.

The game that became known as Exquisite Corpse began with the pattern of a simple transitive sentence. In French, in which adjectives typically follow nouns and in which all nouns are preceded by an article that must agree with the noun in gender and number, the structure is as follows, so that the paper is folded at each slash: subject *article-*

noun / adjective modifying that noun (the gender and number of the noun were the "trailing lines" given as clues to the next writer) / *verb* / object *article-noun / adjective*. (A preposition could be inserted between the verb and the second noun to make the object indirect.) The game could thus involve five players.

One of the first sentences discovered in this way was *Le cadavre / exquis / boira / le vin / nouveau* — "The exquisite corpse will drink the new wine." This beautiful and mysterious sentence, which gave the Surrealists the title for their game, has resonated in my mind for decades. Recently, this resonance found a correlate in the cabalistic figure of Adam Kadmon, the Divine Cosmic Humanity. This is the same figure called by Gnostics the *Anthropos*, whose Fall into separation (first of subject from object, then of all beings from Being) creates the broken universe in which we live. The universe of time and space is the nightmare-ridden death-sleep of the Cosmic Human. When the *Anthropos* heals (becomes whole), says one Gnostic tradition, we will awaken into true, unitary reality; and every step we take beyond the limits of sense-defined, ego-bound separation is part of that awakening.

This double resonance led me to a third: the prophetic poetry of my teacher and friend in eternity William Blake, and especially *The Book of Urizen, The Four Zoas*, and *Milton*, in which the influence of both Cabala and Gnosticism is evident. Absent these poems and the rest of Blake's oeuvre, the very kind of poem I have attempted here would not have been possible. For the reading of Blake that has got me this far, I am especially indebted to Donald Ault's seminal 1974 *Visionary Physics: Blake's Response to Newton*, though also to the criticism of Northrop Frye, Harold Bloom, Jacob Bronowski, Alicia Ostriker, Susan Douglas, and others. I will single out Ostriker and Douglas in particular for their sympathetic feminist critiques of Blake's male bias. This bias is most evident in the later prophetic poems, notably in Blake's gendering of the original Divine Cosmic Human or *Anthropos*, whom he calls Albion, and the aspects or Zoas that compose this Being. They are said to be androgynous before their Fall and division but are always referred to in the masculine, as their Emanations or visions of reality are always referred to in the feminine.

Without here going into what I believe are the reasons for Blake's error, I have moved to correct it with this version of the Fall and Rise of the Eternal Divine Humanity, whom I have gendered as female to signify Her generative and all-embracing quality as well as to allude to the feminine power that in various spiritual traditions around the world gives order and meaning to the universe. By making this correction, I believe I am acting in Blake's own dialectical spirit, in accord with his view that "Without Contraries is No Progression." I have also followed my teacher in employing current science as part of a visionary and spiritual effort. The poem, then, also like Blake's later poetry, is an address to the problem of *mythopoiesis*, the making of myth, in a scientifically based culture in which truth, and therefore meaning, is contingent and approximate, not "eternal." (Fundamentalisms are another, and profoundly wrong, kind of answer to this mythopoetic quest for cosmic meaning.) That said, my poetic goal, like Blake's, is not to preach doctrine or system but to "rouse the faculties to act," to engender new visions in the reader that surpass my own, and to open the gates of eternity in that reader as in myself.

Most of the poem's other more immediate sources are books about physics, cosmology, and biology written for lay readers. Here is a partial list.

Cohen, Jack, and Ian Stewart. *The Collapse of Chaos*
Darling, David. *Equations of Eternity*
_____, _____. *Life Everywhere*
Davies, Paul. *The Mind of God: The Basis for a Rational Universe*
_____, _____. *The Cosmic Jackpot*
Davies, Peter. *Life As We Do Not Know It*
Dawkins, Richard. *The Ancestor's Tale*
Deutsch, David. *The Fabric of Reality*
Gould, Steven Jay. *The Panda's Thumb*
Greene, Brian. *The Elegant Universe*
Kaku, Michio. *Hyperspace*
_____ _____. *Parallel Worlds*
Smolin, Lee. *The Evolution of the Cosmos*
Thomas, Lewis. *Lives of a Cell: Notes of a Biology Watcher*
Wilson, Edward O. *The Diversity of Life*

Lost Poem

for Sandra

In a dream I wrote a poem in my tattered notebook
addressed to you mon ange sauvage
even as you lay sleeping beside me in the tides of breath
that waking I searched for among the scrawled pages in vain
There were other angels in the dream their wings
feathered with beaten copper standing or pacing
as real as the furniture of its crowded or near-vacant rooms
inhabited also by ghosts with body-masks of cold steam swirling
like the tattoos of cloud warriors fallen on the plains of heaven
In the dream my poem was at war with itself
truth fought against truth singing as they clashed together
like blades of two incompatible forms of matter
from different universes joined by the dream's hidden doors
The angels of my poem cried out as they swung their heavy blades
wounding each other their blood beading into mercury spheres
Their wound astronomy was curdled by imaginary and inhuman bliss
into collisions of dying stars like cars on a peripheral boulevard
making the city circled within it slowly spin on its axis
In my dream the poem's limits announced themselves
like enormous mantids crouching in a cabinet as tall as darkness
whispering to each other and me among the corpses of books
In my dream I tried to tell the story of knowing you
and being known by you mon ange sauvage et lumineuse
your wings slamming like shutters in a gale as you tried to wake me
in the unbounded house but the poem was lost

The Whisper of Eros

The whisper of Eros is heard before He arrives
The sound of reeds trembling in a rising wind
The sound of seafoam yielding to dark sand
The whisper of Eros is a poem heard in a dream
His words take form like virtual photons out
Of silence crowded as the vacuum between stars
And vanish again before they are understood
But not before they are known by the taken heart
And the body fills with a cruel and lovely light

Acknowledgments

The author would like to thank the editors of the following publications in which many of these poems first appeared, as follows:

A For Andromeda: A Poetics	*Prosodia*
Angelology & Demonology	*Facture*
Corridors	*SCAPES*
D.O.A.	*Best American Poetry Blog 2011*
Egg-Head: Portrait in a Landscape	*SCAPES*
Gravity's Angels	*Facture*
Handscape	*SCAPES*
Her Hatred	*Caliban Online*
Immigrants: Eucalyptus	*Amsterdam Review*
In the Center of the Forest: A Topology	*SCAPES*
Jargon	*Facture*
Oración / Prayer	*Mantis*
Painscape	*Newport Review*
Philosophical Panorama	*Nouveau's Midnight Sun: Transcriptions from Golgonooza and Beyond*
Red Venice	*Nouveau's Midnight Sun: Transcriptions from Golgonooza and Beyond*
Spaces Inside Sleep	*Melodeon*
Study in Chinatown, San Francisco `	*Amsterdam Review*
Sweat	*Prosodia*
The Anniversary	*Newport Review*
The Sphere of the Nephilim	*SCAPES*

Adam Cornford immigrated to the United States from England in 1979. Since then, he has lived mostly in California but moved to the Philadelphia area in 2020. Cornford led the Poetics Program at New College of California from 1987 until the college closed in 2008. Today he works as a freelance writer and editor. His poetry has appeared widely in print and on the web, including four full-length poetry collections—Shooting Scripts (1978), Animations (1988), Decision Forest (1998), and Lalia (2021). Other works include Liber Ignis (2013), a serial documentary poem with historical photographs, in collaboration with the printer and book artist Peter Rutledge Koch—and several chapbooks, among them 'Round Midnight (1989), O-Town (2003), Scapes (2010) and Mask Report (2014). He has also written lyrics and libretti for the composer Daniel Steven Crafts, who has set several of his poems. A lineal descendant of Charles Darwin, Cornford focuses strongly on science, notably biology, computer science, quantum physics, and cosmology, in his poetry and thought. He counts William Blake and Surrealism as seminal and continuing influences.

About Chax

Founded in 1984 in Tucson, Arizona, Chax has published more than 240 books in a variety of formats, including hand printed letterpress books and chapbooks, hybrid chapbooks, book arts editions, and trade paperback editions such as the book you are holding. From August 2014 until July 2018 Chax Press resided in Houston-Victoria Center for the Arts. Chax is a nonprofit 501(c)(3) organization which depends on suppport from various government & private funders, and, primarly, from individual donors and readers. In July 2018 Chax Press returned to Tucson, Arizona. Our current address is 1517 North Wilmot Road no. 264, Tucson, Arizona 85712-4410. You can email us at chaxpress@gmail.com.

You may find CHAX at https://chax.org

Text & Display: Adobe Caslon Pro

Book Design: Charles Alexander & David Weiss
Book design directed by Charles Alexander
Cover Design: Charles Alexander
Cover Art: Untitled drawing by Christopher Cornford, 1917-1993

Printer & Binder: KC Book Manufacturing